THE MAXIMS OF WALL STREET

by Mark Skousen

THE MAXIMS OF WALL STREET

"Bears Make Headlines, Bulls Make Money"
A compendium of financial adages,
ancient proverbs, and worldly wisdom

FOURTH EDITION

by Mark Skousen

Copyright © 2016, 2011, by Mark Skousen. All rights reserved.
Forecasts & Strategies, Salem Eagle
300 New Jersey Ave., NW, Suite 500, Washington, D.C. 20001
ISBN 978-1-62157-499-6
Distributed by Perseus Distribution

"Proverbs are short sentences drawn from long and wise experience."
— DON QUIXOTE

"The wisdom of the wise,
and the experiences of the ages,
may be preserved by quotations."
— ISAAC DISRAELI

Dedicated to Donald G. Smith,
Wall Street veteran, worldly philosopher
and freedom fighter

Contents

PREFACE TO FOURTH EDITION

"When I see a good thing going cheap,
I buy a lot of it."
— HETTY GREEN

Norman Vincent Peale once remarked, 'The trouble with most of us is that we would rather be ruined by praise than saved by criticism." If that's true then I guess I've been ruined, because *The Maxims on Wall Street* has been so well received that it warrants a fourth edition. The first numbered edition of 1,000 copies sold out quickly, as did a second and third printing. Now over 21,000 copies are in print.

It feels great to write a book that brings people together. I don't think I've received a single complaint except to point out that I should have included this or that quotation.

I sent a review copy to Warren Buffett, considered by many to be the world's greatest investor. I had met him the year before but didn't expect a response. To my surprise, he sent me an email: "Loved your great little book. In fact, I plan to shamelessly steal some of the lines." No doubt his endorsement was affected by the fact that he is quoted the most (28 times), more than Jesse Livermore, Barnard Baruch, Gerald Loeb, Ben Franklin, or Sir John Templeton.

Jack Bogle, the legendary founder of Vanguard group of funds, also wrote a warm handwritten note. "What a treat. It's great to have all these quotes in a single spot." He added three new sayings for the second edition.

Barron's recommended it as the ideal Father's Day gift: "A cogent collection of quotations from the investing giants, phrasemakers, and chroniclers on the beguiling, heartless, and trying ways of Wall Street....a diverting reference for an avid investor or market-history buff."

The *Barron's* review caused Amazon.com to sell out its inventory and the entire first edition.

Stockbrokers, money managers, and investment bankers have ordered multiply copies for their clients and subscribers, and I'm not surprised. It's the perfect gift for students of the market. Following the advice of Hetty Green (see quote above), I offered a special discount for buyers who wanted multiple copies, and they responded. Frank Holmes, president of US Funds in San Antonio, bought a thousand copies for his shareholders, and Brian Wesbury, chief economist at First Trust Advisors of Chicago, ordered 10,000 copies for its clients. (We offer a special discount if you order 100 or more copies.) Hundreds of my subscribers have bought extra copies for friends and relatives, and some even bought a whole box or two. Rodolfo Milani, managing director of Dominick & Dominick of Miami, Florida, wrote, "I find them to be ideal gifts for my best clients."

Dennis Gartman, editor of the *Gartman Letter*, likes the book so much that he keeps it on his desk and draws a quote or two whenever he needs to fill in his newsletter. Last year he was the keynote speaker at the annual CFA dinner in Vancouver, Canada, and when asked what for an appropriate gift for the 700 investment professionals in attendance, he recommended *Maxims*.

Many readers have written to tell me how much depth of wisdom and even humor they have found in *Maxims*. It's been a fun and rewarding exercise. As Alex Green wrote in a review, "*Maxims* is a crash course in how to survive and profit in today's volatile market."

Some readers wonder why I didn't write a brief commentary or tell a story illustrating each proverb or saying. Actually, I'm doing that in every monthly issue of my newsletter, *Forecasts & Strategies*. For example, in the most recent May issue, I highlighted the old Wall Street rule, "Sell in May, and go away." Good advice most of the time!

In another issue, a subscriber complained about a recommended stock that has fallen 20%. In response, I quoted one of Jack Bogle's lines, "If you have trouble imagining a 20% loss in the market, you shouldn't be in stocks." (Fortunately, that stock has since recovered. As Jesse Livermore reminds us, "It takes time to make money.")

And there've been plenty of opportunities lately to remind subscribers that "bears make headlines, bulls make money." Or J. P. Morgan's famous words, "Troubled waters make for good fishing." Or for newsletter writers, "To err is human, but to be paid for it is divine."

I want to thank all my readers and subscribers who have contributed additional sayings for this third edition. Keep them coming for future editions. (My email address is markskousen@skousenpub.com).

Yours for peace, prosperity and liberty, AEIOU,

— MARK SKOUSEN

INTRODUCTION

"We should treat market truisms with respect but not as gospel."

— Dick Davis

"Bears make headlines, bulls make money." Since the spring of 1982, I've been collecting a list of old Wall Street chestnuts, proverbs, slogans, poems, and aphorisms, drawing from experiences in the marketplace and reading dozens of books about Wall Street lore and legend. Whatever you call them, these sayings are daily food for thought on Wall Street, and can teach you a lot about investing.

Some axioms are trite and obvious ("buy low, sell high"), others are profound and thought-provoking ("Nobody is more bearish than a sold-out bull"), a few are mysterious in their meaning ("when history repeats itself, the price goes up"), and some contradict each

1

other (Nicholas Davas says "The only sound reason for my buying a stock is that it is rising in price" and Warren Buffett responds, "The dumbest reason idea in the world is to buy a stock because it's going up in price"). Some are cynically humorous: "Definition of obscene profits: Something you always hear about, but never experience yourself." I've put an asterisk next to my favorite quotations.

Interspersed between these adages are pithy slogans and guideposts expressed by famous investors and money managers such as J. Paul Getty, Benjamin Graham, Jesse Livermore, Russell Sage, Philip Fisher, Warren Buffett, and Richard Russell.

I'd like to think that readers will gain insights into investment and managing their portfolios by following these wise words of wisdom and advice. Many are profound and worthy of long contemplation.

One of my pastimes is to collect rare financial books which often contain the maxims and lore of Wall Street legends. In his book, *How to Be Rich*, J. Paul Getty calls collecting art, including rare books, the "finest investment," one that teaches invaluable lessons in life and makes you more well rounded.

I have collected a number of first editions in the financial field, many of them with intriguing titles or written by famous financiers and speculators. One of my favorites is Henry Clews' 1,000-page tome, *Fifty Years on Wall Street*. The book includes the biographies of many characters on Wall Street during the turn of the 19th century. It had not only been a good investment, appreciating over the years, but is full of wisdom and anecdotes.

In 2009, I presented Richard Russell a new version of "Fifty Years on Wall Street," a compilation of copies of his newsletter, "The Dow Theory Letters," after fifty years of publishing. Dick is a collector of old Wall Street sayings. So is my old friend Jim Dines, editor of *The Dines Letter* since 1960.

Another classic is Yale Professor Irving Fisher's little book, *The Stock Market Crash and After*, published in 1930. Fisher was the most famous economist of the 1920s, was a millionaire, and taught at Yale. He became infamous by suggesting that stocks had reached a "permanent plateau" a week before the crash in October, 1929. After the crash, he opined in his book that the market would recover soon. It didn't, and Fisher was wiped out.

One of the fringe benefits of collecting old financial books is to discover oddly or humorously titled books. Some of my favorites are:

- *I Like the Depression*, by Henry Ansley, "Jackass of the Plains," an autobiography of a well-to-do businessman who was wiped out during the depression and rediscovered his wife, friends, relatives, his dog, and the things that really mattered in life. Not surprisingly, I have the first edition because it's the only edition.

- *How to Retire Without Money*, by Bob Belmont. It takes the author 318 pages to explain his system. It might go well with another book, *Don't Die Broke!,* by Melvin Jay Swartz.

- *How to Live Beyond Your Means*, by Margery Wilson, a delightful book on how to accomplish more with your limited means. It's actually a serious book with several useful suggestions.

- *Wiped Out: How I Lost a Fortune in the Stock Market While the Averages Were Making New High*, by an Anonymous Investor (Simon & Schuster, 1966). A real-life story of a man who entrusted his father's inheritance to irresponsible brokers and lost everything between 1957 and 1964, when the Dow rose 70%.

My most prized possession is a first edition of Roger Babson's autobiography, *Action and Reaction*. Babson is the famed financial guru who predicted the 1929 crash. The book is signed, "Christmas Greetings, 1935, Roger W.

Babson." I also have a collection of the first editions of the hard-money books published during the 1960s and 1970s, including books by authors Harry Browne, Donald J. Hoppe, James Dines, Harry Schultz, Howard Ruff, Jerome Smith, and Doug Casey.

Over the years, I've read a number of classic books in the field, such as:

Reminiscences of a Stock Operator, by Edwin LeFevre, a thinly disguised biography of Jesse Livermore, the speculator king of Wall Street in the early 20th century.

Where are the Customers' Yachts?, or a Good Hard Look at Wall Street, by Fred Schwed Jr.

I've drawn from all these books in collecting old and true adages and axioms for investors.

Unfortunately, it's almost impossible to track down the original source for most old sayings on Wall Street. The original sources are simply forgotten, or repeated so often that it's impossible to know who originated the phrase. For a few well-known statements, I've listed the person who said it first, or the historical context when they were made by Baron Rothschild, Cornelius Vanderbilt, or other famous character.

I would also like to extend my appreciation to Alexander Green, Richard Band, Doug Casey, Ken Fisher, Adrian Day, Rick Rule, Bob Bishop, John Templeton, Martin Truax, Gary Alexander, Dennis Slothower, Linda Oleson, Wendell Brock, Rich Whelan, Jim Rogers, Tom Hudson, Rolf White, Steve Forbes, Bill Bonner, Dennis Gartman, Ron Holland, Jim Dines, Richard Russell, Dick Davis, Donald Smith, Bill Henry, Mark Tier, Bert Dohmen, Yale Hirsch, Howard Eynon, Ralph Williams, Richard Southwell, John Steele Gordon and many others who helped in making suggestions for this compilation. I especially want to thank Fraser Books of Burlingame, Vermont, which publishes a catalog of dozens of old-time financial books, and all the old dusty bookstores that I have frequented over the years in search of financial wisdom.

Normally, I thank my wife Jo Ann for her extraordinary editing skills, but in this case, she says I don't need any help with cliches.

In liberty, AEIOU,

Mark Skousen
New York, New York

Special Note to All Readers

I hesitate to subtitle this book "The Complete List of Wall Street Sayings." No doubt I have missed some of your favorite rules, adages, and proverbs. If you find an old Wall Street adage, short poem, or pithy sentence that I've missed, please send it to me at markskousen@skousenpub.com and I'll add it to the next edition.

A Tale of the Broker

"Bull markets are born on pessimism,
grow on skepticism, mature on optimism,
and die on euphoria."
— JOHN TEMPLETON

Wall Street was in an ebullient, happy mood. Stocks were in a major bull market for the first time in years. Prices were rising practically every day. As a new investor, I wanted to participate in the big money, so I decided to take the plunge.

My wise Uncle Ervin counseled me, "You can't make big money without taking big risks," but I liked my chances.

A friend at work had recommended investing in a small company called "Little Gamble, Inc." So I called my stockbroker, Claude Twindledumb, and said resolutely, "I would like to buy 100 shares of Little Gamble."

My broker gasped. "When the wind blows

even the turkeys will fly."

"What?" I asked perplexed.

"A rising tide will float all boats."

"Oh?" I said, still confused. Wall Street sure has a strange way of talking.

"What I mean is," explained Claude, "Little Gamble is a lousy stock. It's fine during a bull market like now, but it will crash like a rocket when the market heads south."

He paused, then advised, "Besides, don't put all your eggs in one basket. Why don't you buy a group of stocks for diversification? I recommend Jitterbug, a well-diversified mutual fund. It has a good track record and is bound to move up with the market."

"How much is it?"

"Five dollars a share."

I bought the fund, and happily, it quickly rose to $6, which was pretty good for a mutual fund. Then it went up to $7. I was in seventh heaven. I called Uncle Erv, who suggested I take some profits. He would often say, "Remember, nephew, trees don't grow to the sky. When a pig becomes a hog, he gets slaughtered." But I wasn't listening. I was just getting started and it was too much fun to sell out that soon.

I called broker Claude, and said, "You know that stock fund, Jitterbug, that I bought from you....I think I should buy some more."

The broker nodded. "Past performance is no guarantee of future profits, but the market still looks good. I always say, don't fight the tape. Let your profits run." So I purchased 100 more shares.

But then quite unexpectedly the market took a dive, and Jitterbug fell to $6 ½. I called my broker and expressed concern.

"Should I sell and take my profits?"

"Well, son, you never lose money by taking a profit," Claude advised. "But I don't recommend selling at this time. Bull markets climb a wall of worry. Relax, it's a bull-market correction. Hold on, it will turn around.

Patience in market is worth pounds in a year."

"What was that?" I didn't quite understand, but I was comforted, at least temporarily. Unfortunately, however, the market kept dropping and now was in a full-scale retreat. Soon Jitterbug was below $5, my original buy price. I was getting nervous again, and called my broker Claude.

"You know that stock fund you sold me," I began, but the broker cut me off.

"Know value, not prices," Claude said philosophically. "The long run outlook for Jitterbug is excellent. Don't worry about a short-term depression in the market."

I wasn't completely comfortable with his words, but what was I to do? After all, in the land of the blind, the one-eyed is king.

Notwithstanding, the market saw things differently, and it wasn't long before the price of Jitterbug fell to $3 a share. At this point, I was resigned to my losses. "I've lost so much already, there's no point is selling, I might as well hold on until it turns around," I said to myself. My broker agreed. "It's a good time to dollar-cost average by purchasing more shares. When the market recovers, you'll have an instant profit."

I'm not sure what he meant, but I followed his advice, and bought a few more shares as the price dropped. And boy did it drop. Wall Street was now in a major bear market (a term used by my broker), and it wasn't long before Jitterbug dropped to a buck.

Frankly, I was fed up, sick and tired of holding on and seeing my account decline in value practically every day. I might lose my entire investment. One day I reached the break point. I was determined to get rid of this lousy fund.

But before I called my broker, I talked to Uncle Erv. I was surprised by his attitude. "Nephew, it's good you lost some money. It's not good to make money on your first trade— you think investing is easy." Then he added,

"You bought at the top. Don't compound the error by selling at the bottom." He had the gall to recommend buying instead of selling. He said something about buying straw hats in January, but I didn't get his meaning.

"Buy on mystery, sell on history. When the public is selling, it's time to buy," he counseled.

But I was in no mood to listen. I called Twindledumb and demanded, "Sell! I don't want to hear any of your arguments. Just get me out of Jitterbug, no questions asked." The broker executed my order dutifully, and I finally sold out at $1 a share.

The only consolation my broker could give me was, "Cheer up. The worst thing that can happen to a new investor is to make money on his first trade. You'll do better next time."

"Yeah, I've heard that before," I said.

And right he was. The market finally started to move up again. Jitterbug rose to $2. Damn! Out of curiosity, I called my broker to see what he thought. "Just a bear-market rally," he said.

"Don't throw good money after bad."

Gee, I was surprised that my broker was as bearish as I was. Nonetheless, the market has a mind of its own and kept rising. Jitterbug went to $3. Now it seemed that the stock market recovery was for real. I called Claude, but he was pessimistic.

"It's too late now. You should have bought at $1 or $2. Now it's no longer a bargain. But don't worry. You can't kiss all the pretty girls. Fortunately, there's more than one way to climb a mountain. A new train leaves the station every ten minutes. I'm sure another good investment opportunity with come along shortly. Let's be patient and stay liquid. After all, you never lose money standing aside."

It was sound advice, I thought, but I was still itching to make a profit in the marketplace. "Buy cheap, sell dear," wasn't that the object? It was harder than I thought. The final blow came several weeks later. Jitterbug climbed to $5, the price I had started with a year ago. Wall Street was back on top, and shouldn't I be part of it?

I figured if it was a good buy at $5, it must be even better now. I called my broker and said, "I'm tired of taking your advice. Buy Jitterbug and don't talk me out of it."

After going through all this, I'm not sure I'm any better at investing. I noticed that the stock fund Jitterbug recently was selling for $4 a share. My broker is always helpful, though. He says, "You have to kiss a lot of frogs before finding a prince." I suppose he's right. But my wise old Uncle Erv probably said it best when he told me that a broker is, more than anything, often in error but seldom in doubt.

OLD WALL STREET SAYINGS
and
WORLDLY WISDOM

SAVING, INVESTING AND SPENDING

"No man is so harmlessly occupied
as when he is making money."
— SAMUEL JOHNSON

"Better that a man should tyrannize over his
bank balance than over his fellow-citizens."
— JOHN MAYNARD KEYNES

"Any earner who earns more than he can
spend is automatically an investor."
— GERALD LOEB

"Two of the hardest things to do
is save when you're young
and spend when you're old."
— UNKNOWN

"Frugality is a handsome income."
— ERASMUS, 1459-1536

"Economy is a great source of revenue."
— SENECA

"Shake the apple tree,
but don't cut the limbs."
— ANONYMOUS

"Don't eat the fruit
while the tree is in blossom."
— BENJAMIN DISRAELI

"If your financial house is in order,
you can afford to be patient."
— ROBERT BISHOP

"The poor and middle class work for money.
The rich have money work for them."
— ROBERT KIYOSAKI

"If you marry a rich man, beware: either they
don't stay rich, or they don't stay married."
— TERRY SAVAGE

"If you want to get rich, go into finance."
— ROBERT SHILLER

"A Part of All You Earn is Yours to Keep"

"In old Babylon there once lived a certain very rich man named Arkad. Far and wide he was famed for his great wealth. Also was he famed for his liberality. He was generous with his charities. He was generous with his family. He was liberal in his own expenses. But nevertheless each year his wealth increased more rapidly than he spent it."

Why? Because, Arkad said,
"A part of all you earn is yours to keep."
— GEORGE S. CLASON
"The Richest Man in Babylon"

"If you want to be wealthy,
live below your means."
— PAUL MERRIMAN

"Save a lot and save often."
— RICHARD BERNSTEIN

"One of the dumbest things you can do
with money is spend it."
—— ROBERT WILSON
(short seller)

"Save as much as you can and
your investments will do better."
—— JOHN E. CORE

"When your outgo exceeds your income,
your upkeep becomes your downfall."
—— RICK RULE

"The more I make, the more I spend.
I don't want to die rich."
—— JESSE LIVERMORE

"Any man can earn a dollar,
but it takes a wise man to keep it."
—— RUSSELL SAGE

"Most of the great investors are misers."
—— JOHN TRAIN
The Money Masters

How to Make a Million

"How do you make a million?
Start with $2 million."
— OLD COMMODITY TRADER LINE

"How do you become a millionaire?
Start with $1 billion and buy an airline."
— RICHARD BRANSON, *Virgin Air*

"Marry a millionaire, or better yet,
divorce one."
— *FORBES*

"How do you make a million?
Start with $900,000."
— STEPHEN LEWIS

"How do you make a million?
Borrow a million, and pay it off."
– JACK MILLER
real estate tycoon

Rich Man's Pearl of Wisdom #1
Story of a Rich Doctor

Several years ago, a medical doctor practicing in New York City came to see me for a consultation. He was in the top of his field, and making at the time a half million dollars a year. Yet he faced serious financial problems. He said he was always in debt and had a hard time paying his bills. He blamed his troubles on a variety of factors — high wages and benefits he had to pay his employees, high New York City taxes, malpractice insurance premiums, and his wife's spending habits. He wanted my advice on how to overcome this constant problem. "I'll spend two days with you, if necessary," he told me over the telephone.

The traditional approach to this man's problem would normally take several days to analyze. A financial planner would want to look at the doctor's tax returns, net worth statements, and budget. But my method could be called "Financial Planning Made Easy." It took less than an hour to explain.

"Your problem, doctor, is that you are paying everyone else before you pay yourself."

He looked baffled, so I explained further. "Every month you pay the landlord, the water company, the utility company, the bank, the city of New York, your employees, and your wife. Then you keep what's left over, except that nothing is left over."

"That's right!" he responded.

I urged him to reverse the order. "Pay yourself first," I admonished. I instructed him to write out a check for $2,000 at the first of the month, before he pays any other bills, wages, even taxes, and put that money in a brokerage account and invest it in a mutual fund or any other investment he liked.

"That's all there is to it?" he asked with a pained look on his face.

"That's it, nothing more," I said. He paid

my one-hour consulting fee and left my office with a puzzled look, doubting that it would solve his problem.

I had practically forgotten about this consultation until a year later when the doctor called me on the telephone. He refreshed my memory and told me what happened. He seemed to be angry. "Funny thing, Mr. Skousen, nothing has changed since I met you a year ago. I'm still struggling to pay my bills, taxes are going up, my wife keeps spending like crazy, and my employees want a raise."

He concluded, "So you see, Mr. Skousen, your system didn't work at all."

But then he paused and said this: "Oh, one more thing: I now have $24,000 sitting in my brokerage account. What should I do with this money?"

The New York doctor was flabbergasted that somehow, despite all odds, my simple system was working. He had become a follower of what I call the Automatic Wealth Builder.

Where did the extra $24,000 come from? Frankly, I don't know, and neither does the doctor. This technique works because of the psychology of personal finance. People don't spend money they don't see. Budgets adjust almost automatically to the new subconscious pressure to reduce wasteful expenditures.

The system is simple but effective: Put savings first. As George S. Clason says in *The Richest Man in Babylon*: "A part of all you earn is yours to keep."

Market Timing

"When the facts change, I change my mind.
What do you do, sir?"
— JOHN MAYNARD KEYNES

"I hate to be wrong.
But I hate more to stay wrong."
— PAUL A. SAMUELSON

"The difference between a rich investor
and a poor investor is the quality —
and timeliness — of his information."
— BERNARD BARUCH

"We cannot direct the wind,
but we can adjust the sail."
— ANON

"A mariner does not become skilled
by always sailing on a calm sea."
— HEBER J. GRANT

"If you can't be the first, be the second."
— JESSE LIVERMORE

"Success rides on the hour of decision."
— JESSE LIVERMORE

"Buying at the bottom and selling at the top
are typically done by liars."
— BERNARD BARUCH

"The market does what it should do,
but not always when."
— JESSE LIVERMORE

"They don't ring a bell
when the market turns."
— OLD WALL STREET AXIOM

"They don't ring a bell when it's time to sell."
— BILL HENRY

"Never mind telling me *what* stocks to buy;
tell me *when* to buy them."
— HUMPHREY NEILL

"Investments are like anniversaries.
You can't be a day late."
— AD FOR SPDRs

Bargain Hunting

"Necessity never made a good bargain."
— BEN FRANKLIN

"Even the best company
with the best prospects should
be bought at a reasonable price."
— DICK DAVIS

"The smart investor must know the difference
between what is *temporarily* undervalued
and what is *permanently* undervalued."
— JOHN TEMPLETON

"When I talk to a company that tells me
the last analyst showed up three years ago,
I can hardly contain my enthusiasm."
— PETER LYNCH

"Buy cats [cheap and timely securities],
not dogs."
— GABE WISDOM

Nothing can make the spirit fly higher
Than finding a bargain when you're the buyer.
And nothing can make the spirit sink deeper
Than finding it later a whole lot cheaper.*
— submitted by
WENDELL BROCK

"The public is fearful of bargains."
— J. PAUL GETTY

"The best investments are often those that
look dead wrong when they are made."
— MAXIM ON WALL STREET

"Quality is always a bargain."
— LOWELL MILLER

"Buy *fallen* angels, not *falling* angels."
— GABE WISDOM

BUY CHEAP, SELL DEAR
A Variation on a Theme

"Buy cheap, sell dear."
— BARON ROTHSCHILD

"Buy good stocks cheap."
— JOEL GREENBLATT

"It is next to impossible to know what is 'cheap' and what is 'dear' in stock prices."
— GERALD LOEB

"Cheap stocks are not always bargains."
— ASMATH DAMODARAN

"Today's version of 'Buy low, sell high': Buy high, sell higher. Stocks that are high and going higher are a good buy. Stocks that are 'cheap' and growing cheaper don't interest me."
— GERALD LOEB
Battle for Investment Survival

"It's easier to buy high and sell higher
than to buy low and sell high."
— JIM DINES

"There is no secret in fortune making.
I believe in getting in at the bottom
and out at the top. All you have to do is
buy cheap and sell dear, act with thrift and
shrewdness and be persistent. When I see a
good thing going cheap because nobody wants
it, I buy a lot of it and tuck it away."
— HETTY GREEN
"The Witch of Wall Street"

"Sell low, buy lower."
(short seller version)

"The stock market is the only place where
the customers don't buy when
the merchandise goes on sale."
— ALEX GREEN

"A great business at a fair price is superior
to a fair business at a great price."
— CHARLIE MUNGER'S #1 LESSON OF INVESTING

"Our investments are chosen
on the basis of value, not popularity."
— WARREN BUFFETT
Letter to Shareholders

"Nothing grows in the shadow of an oak tree."
— T. ROWE PRICE

"If a stock is a good investment at $20,
it's a steal at $10."
— HOWARD GOLD

"Buy stocks like socks – good quality on sale."
— FORBES

"It's not what you buy.
It's how much you pay for it."
— CARL ICAHN

Contrary Investing

"It is contrary to one's natural reactions
to be contrary to general opinions."
— HUMPHREY B. NEILL
The Art of Contrary Thinking

"No one can possibly achieve any real
and lasting success or 'get rich'
in business by being a conformist."
— J. PAUL GETTY

"Bull markets are born on pessimism, grow on
skepticism, mature on optimism, and die on
euphoria. The time of maximum pessimism
is the best time to buy, and time of maximum
optimism is the best to time to sell."
— JOHN TEMPLETON

"Don't buy what's hot — buy what's not."
— RICK RULE

"It's better in the Bahamas"

"My job was being paid by wealthy families to
help them choose stocks and bonds. And my
results were much better when I was working
from here than from Manhattan, Radio City
and Rockefeller Center. I had good results in
New York. But when I came here, I had better
results. The secret, I think, is that in order to
buy stocks at a bargain price, you have to do
the opposite of the crowd. When you're going
to the same meetings with the other people in
Manhattan, it's hard to be different."

—JOHN TEMPLETON
QUOTED IN 'ADAM SMITH,' *THE MONEY GAME*

"I always gave the public what they wanted.
When the public wanted stock, I gave them
my stock. When the public wants out,
I took the stock back."

— BERNARD BARUCH

"Unless volatility is extremely low
or very high one should think twice
about betting against the crowd."
— Shawn Andrew

"If the baby wakes up, it gets fed."
— Unknown

"When the ducks quack, you feed them."
— Anonymous
(When the market is strong, you sell.)

"When everyone is thinking the same way,
nobody is thinking."
— General George Patton, Jr.

"When everyone is a contrarian,
nobody is a contrarian!"
— Mark Skousen

"Do you want to be a contrarian or a victim?
The choice is yours."
— Rick Rule

"The stock market is inherently deceptive.
Doing what everyone else is doing…
is often the wrong thing to do."
— Philip Fisher

"Be fearful when others are greedy
and greedy when others are fearful."
— WARREN BUFFETT

"Young man, always have greed
when others have fear
and have fear when others have greed."
— ROY NEUBERGER

"Invest at the point of maximum pessimism."
— JOHN TEMPLETON

"The dissenter is every human being
at those moments of his life
when he resigns momentarily
from the herd and thinks for himself."
— ARCHIBALD MACLEISH

"Worldly wisdom teaches that it is better
for reputation to fail conventionally
then to succeed unconventionally."
— JOHN MAYNARD KEYNES

"When it's dark enough,
you can see the stars."
— OLD PERSIAN SAYING

"Where the sun is the brightest,
the shade is the deepest."
— WALTER SAVAGE LANDOR

"Buy when blood is running in the streets."
— BARON ROTHSCHILD

"The problem with being an early contrarian
is that the blood in the streets is often your own."
— RON MILLER

"If Wall Street hates a stock, buy it."
— MARTIN SOSNOFF

"Buy on the sound of the cannon,
sell on the sound of the trumpets [cornets]."
— BARON ROTHSCHILD

"Buy on mystery, sell on history."
— OLD WALL STREET SAW

"It is wiser to be early than to be late…
A contrary opinion is usually
ahead of its time."
— HUMPHREY B. NEILL

"Buy at the wake, sell at the wedding."
— AL GOLDMAN (A. G. Edwards)

"Only a fool holds out for top dollar"

J oe Kennedy was a strict contrarian. He had an ideal temperament for speculating — "a passion for facts, a complete lack of sentiment, a marvelous sense of timing," as a confidante once said. According to various accounts, Kennedy stayed in the market until late 1928, when he sold most of his RKO "A" shares, netting several million dollars. He spent the 1928-29 winter at his second home in Palm Beach, Florida, where he purchased his estate at a bargain price after the Florida real estate crash.

Kennedy was tempted to get back into the market in early 1929, but in the summer, when he saw that shoeshine boys were talking about hot stocks, he decided against it. "Only a fool holds out for top dollar." As biographer Richard Whelan wrote, "Then and there, so ran his recollection, he decided that a market anyone could play, and a shoeshine boy could predict, was no market for him."

Bernard Baruch said much the same thing: "When beggars and shoeshine boys, barbers and beauticians can tell you how to get rich it is time to remind yourself that there is no more dangerous illusion than the belief that one can get something for nothing."

———

"Buy when everyone else is selling
and hold until everyone else is buying.
This is more than just a catchy slogan.
It is the very essence of successful investing."
— J. Paul Getty

"Buy on weakness, sell on strength."
— Michael D. Sheimo

"The public is right during the trends but
wrong at both ends."*
— Humphrey Neill
The Art of Contrary Thinking

"When you're tickled to death, sell.
Scared to death, buy."
— ERNIE WILLIAMS

"When they're yellin', you should be sellin'
When they're cryin', you should be buyin'.*
— MARILYN COHEN

"Buy into extreme weakness,
sell into extreme strength."
— ANONYMOUS

"If you wait to see the Robin sing,
Spring may be over."*
— WARREN BUFFETT

"Buy straw hats in the winter, when nobody
wants them, and sell them in the summer
when everybody needs them."
— RUSSELL SAGE

"If you hear that everybody is buying a certain
stock, ask who is selling."
— JAMES DINES

"Trees don't grow to the sky."
— ANONYMOUS

"The more certain something is,
the less likely it is to be profitable."
— JIM ROGERS

"Unless there's fear in buying a stock,
you can't make big money."
— ROBERT WILSON

"It is the one sphere of life and activity where
victory, security and success are always to the
minority and never to the majority.
When you find any one agreeing with you,
change your mind.
When I can persuade the Board of my
Insurance Company to buy a share,
that, I am learning from experience,
is the right moment for selling it."
— JOHN MAYNARD KEYNES (1937)

"You can't buy what is popular and do well."
— WARREN BUFFETT

"Being contrary doesn't relieve you
from the obligation of thinking!"
— RICHARD BAND

"No price is too high to pay for RCA."
— GROWTH STOCK SLOGAN IN THE LATE 1920S

"It's better to be a pirate
than to join the navy."
— STEVE JOBS

Benjamin Graham on Mr. Market

"Mr. Market comes along each day quoting you a variety of prices for assets. He will buy or sell at the quoted price. Often his quotes reflect fair value. Mr. Market is, however, a manic depressive. On some occasions he is depressed and he prices assets too cheaply. Other days he's unreasonably optimistic and his prices are too high. The contrarian's job is to go investing when Mr. Market is depressed and to divest when he's unreasonably optimistic."

— BENJAMIN GRAHAM
The Intelligent Investor

Mario Gabelli on Cash Flow

"We believe the best barometer of a company's value is free cash flow: How much cash is this business throwing off today and how much is he going to have to invest in this business to grow this stream of cash in the future."

— MARIO GABELLI

Risk and Reward

"Great estates may venture more;
little boats must keep near shore."
— BEN FRANKLIN

"He that would catch fish,
must venture his bait."
— BEN FRANKLIN

"Fish see the bait, but not the hook;
men see the profit, but not the peril."
— OLD CHINESE PROVERB

"You have to go out on a limb sometimes
because that's where the nuts are."
— WILL ROGERS

"Easy money — isn't."
— KEN FISHER

"The easy money has already been made."
— BILL HENRY'S MOST HATED ADAGE

"Everyone has the brainpower to make money
in stocks. Not everyone has the stomach."
— PETER LYNCH

"I don't believe in taking foolish chances,
but nothing can be accomplished
without taking any chance at all."
— CHARLES LINDBERGH

"Hasty climbers have sudden falls."
— JIM DAVIDSON

"The stock market isn't a free market,
it's a free for all."
— DIEGO VIETIA

"Those who try to make a killing
usually get killed."
— JULIAN SNYDER

"Risk taking is necessary for large success —
but it is also necessary for failure."
— NASSIM TALEB

"Investors should purchase stocks
like they purchase groceries —
not like they purchase perfume."
— BEN GRAHAM

"How many insecurities traded
on Wall Street today?"
— FRANZ PICK

"October: This is one of the peculiarly
dangerous months to speculate in stocks.
The others are July, January, September, April,
November, May, March, June, December,
August and February."
— MARK TWAIN

"If the price is low enough, there is a
substantial margin of safety."
— BEN GRAHAM

"The way to be safe is to never feel secure."
— JIM DAVIDSON

"It is often a long road to quick profits."*
— HUMPHREY NEILL

"You can't make big money
without taking big risks."
— ANONYMOUS

"If you can't take the sting,
don't reach for the honey."
— UNKNOWN

"Tall trees catch much wind."
— ANONYMOUS

"The worst thing that can happen to an
investor is to make money on his first trade.
He thinks investing is easy."
— MARK SKOUSEN

"If you want to see a rainbow,
you have to stand a little rain."*
— JIMMY DURANTE

"Better to be a crooked furrow
than a field unplowed."
— PAUL JEWKES

"Where there's beauty, there's danger."
— HELEN MCCARTY

"Think risk first, then reward."
— ANTHONY M. GALLEA

Dancing Down Wall Street

"Until the music stops,
you gotta keep dancing."
— CHUCK PRINCE

"When the music stops,
you better have a chair."
— BARRY STERNLICHT
(Starwood Hotels)

"The dance down Wall Street isn't random,
it's a waltz."
— KEN FISHER

"But is it a Tennessee waltz
or a Viennese waltz?"
— MARK SKOUSEN

"The market can do anything."
— JESSE LIVERMORE

"I am more concerned about the return *of* my principal than the return *on* my principal."
— WILL ROGERS

"There are few things in investing that are more important than preservation of capital."
— DICK DAVIS

"He will risk half his fortune in the stock market with less reflection than he devotes to the selection of a medium-priced automobile."
— EDWIN LEFEVRE

"Always ask 'How much money can you stand to lose?'"
— DONALD TRUMP

"Wild traders may make it on Wall Street, but they rarely keep it."
— KEN FISHER

"Take calculated risks, but don't be rash."
— GEORGE PATTON JR.

"The market takes no prisoners."
— OLD WALL STREET SAYING

"The most dangerous game of modern society
is the hunt for money."
— JULIAN M. SNYDER

"He that lives by the sword dies by the sword."
— MATTHEW 26:52

"When in doubt, err on the side of safety."
— HARRY BROWNE

"Don't gamble. Take all your savings and buy
some good stock and hold it till it goes up,
then sell it. If it don't go up, don't buy it."
— WILL ROGERS

"Without sell offs, there are no rallies."
— AL FRANK (The Prudent Speculator)

"When you want to test the depths of a
stream, don't use both feet."
— CHINESE PROVERB

"Fast ripe, fast rotten."
— JAPANESE PROVERB

"Buying Treasuries isn't investing.
It's out-vesting."
— CNBC COMMENTATOR

Leverage and Debt

"You don't launch spaceships
with firecrackers."
— BOB ALLEN

"Leverage is like shooting an arrow into the
air. Eventually it comes down to earth."
— MARK SKOUSEN

"Heavily margined, heavily watched."
— MICHAEL SHEIMO

"He who lives by leverage, dies by leverage."
— KEN FISHER

"It takes courage to ride with huge leverage.
It takes courage to be a pig."
— GEORGE SOROS

Crisis and Speculating

"Troubled waters makes for good fishing."*
— DANIEL DREW
based on the old Latin proverb
"In aqua turbida piscatur uberius."

"A smooth sea never made a skilled mariner."
— OLD SAILOR'S PROVERB

"The speculators, the in-and-outers,
are the stabilizers of the market.
They are the life-savers, the necessary evil."
— JESSE LIVERMORE

Predicting the Future

"It is better to be approximately right
than precisely wrong."
— JOHN MAYNARD KEYNES

"The price of being right is first being wrong."
— ANONYMOUS

"In the land of the blind,
the one-eyed is king."*
— UNKNOWN

"Stocks will fluctuate."
— J. P. MORGAN

"Black swans, those rare and unexpected
deviations, can be both good and bad events."
— NASSIM TALEB

"The rarer the event the more
undervalued it will be in price."
— NASSIM TALEB

"Better to prepare than to predict."
— HANK BROCK

"The stock market has forecast
nine of the last five recessions."
— Paul A. Samuelson

"The one investment certainty is that
we are all frequently wrong."
— Bill Gross

"A wise trader never ceases
to study general conditions."
— Edwin Lefevre

"If you really know what's going on,
you don't even have to know what's going on
to know what's going on."
— George Goodman
"Adam Smith," *The Money Game*

"If you want to stay ahead,
keep one eye on the Fed."
— Patrick Balogna

"No one can see ahead three years,
let alone five or ten."
— T. Rowe Price

Fear and Greed

"Fear and greed are highly contagious."
— DICK DAVIS

"Discipline, which is but mutual trust
and confidence, is the key to all success
in peace and war."
— GEN. GEORGE S. PATTON, JR.

"Perhaps the foremost lesson which I have
learned is that emotions rule the world, rather
than statistics, information, or anything else."
— ROGER BABSON

"Bull markets climb a wall of worry."
— OLD BROKER SAYING

"Be fearful when others are greedy,
and greedy when others are fearful."
— WARREN BUFFETT

"There are two kinds of fear, fear itself
and fear of being left behind."
— ROBERT CAREY

Animal Farm on Wall Street

"Bulls make money, bears make money,
but hogs go hungry."

"Bulls make money, bears make money,
pigs get slaughtered."

"When a pig becomes a hog,
he gets slaughtered."

"Little pigs get under the fence,
big pigs don't."

"I'm not a bull.
I'm not a bear.
I'm a chicken."

— CHARLES ALLMON
Growth Stock Outlook

"Bubbles always burst."

— UNKNOWN

"Bubbles are invisible
to those inside the bubbles."

— JIM DINES

"Get-rich-quick schemes just don't work.
If they did, then everyone on the face
of the earth would be a millionaire."

— J. PAUL GETTY

"Fear sells better than greed."

— OLD MADISON AVENUE ADAGE

"Definition of obscene profits:
something you've always heard about
but never experienced yourself."

— ANONYMOUS

"Trading stocks is simple mathematics
2 + 2 = 4, but our greed makes it 5
and our panic makes it 3."

— FEROZ AHMED KHAN

"Greed is good."

— GORDON GEKKO, "Wall Street" (1987)

"Sorry, Gekko, but greed isn't good –
look where it landed you [in jail]."

— ANTHONY SCARAMUCCI

Strategies

"There's many ways to climb a mountain."
— UNKNOWN

"To be a successful investor you must draw
from many disciplines."
— CHARLIE MUNGER

"If you take care of the pennies, the dollars
will take care of themselves."
— RUSSELL SAGE

"Women and wine, game and deceit, makes
the wealth small and the wants great."
— BEN FRANKLIN

"Throughout the centuries there were men
who took first steps down new roads armed
with nothing but their own vision."
— AYN RAND

"For best results, the competitive
player should never depart
from his area of expertise."
— JOHN TRAIN
The Money Masters

"Be an owner, not a lender."
— ANTHONY M. GALLEA

"There's nothing wrong with cash.
It gives you time to think."
— ROBERT PRECHTER JR.

"The investor of today does not profit
from yesterday's growth."
— WARREN BUFFETT

"Why not invest your assets in the companies
you really like? As Mae West said, 'Too much
of a good thing can be wonderful.'"
— WARREN BUFFETT

"Double up on winners."
— ANTHONY M. GALLEA

"To resist change is like holding your breath
— if you persist, you will die."
— LAO TSU

"Half the plowing is in the planning."
— ARTHUR CUTTEN

"Always go home with the guy that brung ya."
— PEARL BAILEY
(if an investment works, stay with it.)

"Only a fool thinks he must
trade all the time."
— EDWIN LEFEVRE

"Stocks are never too high for you to begin
buying or too low to begin selling."
— EDWIN LEFEVRE

"You don't need to take the last dollar."
— CHARLIE MUNGER

"There's just as much profit potential
in high-quality stocks as there is
in low-quality stocks."
— GERALDINE WEISS AND JANET LOWE

"Genius is nothing but
a greater aptitude for patience."
— GEORGES LOUIS BUFFON

"Investing without research is like playing
stud poker and never looking at the cards."
— PETER LYNCH

"No pilot, no matter how great his talent
or experience, fails to use his checklist."
— CHARLIE MUNGER

"An investor without investment objectives is
like a traveler without a destination."
— RALPH SEGER

"Buy what you know."
— PETER LYNCH

"You can make excuses and you can make
money, but you cannot make both."
— ZIAD K. ABDELNOUR

Wall Street

"Wall Street is a street with a river at one end
and a graveyard at the other."
— Called a "sinister old gag"
by FRED SCHWED JR.

"Wall Street is a touchstone for the intelligent
and a tombstone for the audacious."
— DON JOSÉ DE LA VEGAS

Brokers, Advisors, and Gurus

"They don't leave any money on the table."
— OLD BROKER LINE

"There's no free lunch on Wall Street."
— UNKNOWN

"For Wall Street, the dumb money pays."
— OLD WALL STREET SAYING

"Copper your customers and grow rich."
— Quoted as "an old and true adage"
by EDWIN LEFEVRE

"If we do well for the client,
we'll be taken care of."
— T. ROWE PRICE

"Whose bread I eat, his song I sing."
— OLD SAYING

"Don't always trust the experts."
— STEVE FORBES

"Even experts can be wrong."
— ANTHONY M. GALLEA

"One of the most dangerous enemies to a
trader is a magnetic personality."
— EDWIN LEFEVRE

"There are clear lines separating those who
swear by him and those who swear at him."
— LOUIS RUKEYSER
on Joe Granville (1981)

"The ones who usually make the biggest
mistakes are those who predict
they will never make a mistake."
— NEWTON ZINDER
(E. F. Hutton)

"If Jack's in love, he's no judge of Jill's beauty."
— BEN FRANKLIN

"I make more money selling advice
than following it."
— MALCOLM FORBES

"I'm often in error, but seldom in doubt."
— IRA COBLEIGH

"To err is human,
but to be paid for it is divine."
— HOWARD RUFF

"Wall Street is the only place that people
ride to in a Rolls Royce to get advice
from those who take the subway."
— WARREN BUFFETT

"The customer only buys winners,
the broker only sells losers."
— AL ROACH

"The broker told me to buy this stock
for my old age. It worked wonderfully.
Within a week I was an old man."
— EDDIE CANTOR

"Never buy anything from someone
who is out of breath."
— BURT MALKIEL

Where Are the Customers' Yachts?

"Once in the dear dead days beyond recall, an out-of-town visitor was being shown the wonders of the New York financial district. When the party arrived at the Battery, one of his guides indicated some handsome ships riding at anchor. He said, 'Look, those are the bankers' and brokers' yachts.'

'Where are the customers' yachts?' asked the naïve visitor."

— FRED SCHWED, JR.
Where are the customers' yachts? (1940)

"The investor is more important
than the investment."
— DICK FABIAN

"Nobody does business with a failure."
— ANONYMOUS

"Success has a thousand fathers,
failure is an orphan."
— BEN FRANKLIN

"In this business, you are either
a hero or a zero."
— DENNIS SLOTHOWER

"Many shall be restored that are now fallen
and many shall fall that are now in honor."
— HORACE

"It is the mountaintop
that the lightning strikes."
— HORACE

"Don't squat with your spurs on."

"I make my own questions and see
with my own eyes.
I have no use for another man's spectacles."
— RUSSELL SAGE
(quoted in *Reminiscences of a Stock Operator*)

"You can cut somebody's hair many times, but you can only scalp him once."

— ANONYMOUS

"Don't ask a barber if you need a haircut."
(brokers are salesman, not objective observers)

"Beware of the prophet seeking profits."

— DENNIS MILLER

"Never invest in God."
(If someone approaches you on an investment and mentioned how religious he is, run.)

"You can't tell till you bet."

— PAT HEARNE
favorite race-track maxim
(quoted in Edwin Lefevre,
Reminiscences of a Stock Operator).

"You have to pet the pony."

— BILL HENRY

"Wall Street has become fabulously successful at separating capital from its owners."
— TED ARONSON

"Brokers can trade for other people, but they can't trade for themselves. They lose their nerve when they handle their own money."
— ARTHUR CUTTEN

"Stockbrokers know the price of everything and the value of nothing."
— PHILIP FISHER

"The more someone wants to sell you an investment the more you shouldn't buy it."
— BILL BONNER

"The business of Wall Street often consists of introducing people who shouldn't buy securities to people who shouldn't sell them."
— UNKNOWN

Humility and Vanity

"The most important lesson in investing
is humility."
— JOHN TEMPLETON

"Wall Street teaches humility."
— OLD SAYING

"Pride preceedeth the fall."
— PROVERBS 16:18

"No price is too high for a speculator to keep
him from getting a swelled head."
— EDWIN LEFEVRE

"The stock doesn't know you own it."
— WALL STREET APHORISM

"Stay humble or the market
will do it for you."
— ANONYMOUS

"The arrogant are blind to the truth."
— JIM ROGERS

"Fools and fanatics are always so certain
of themselves, but wiser people
are so full of doubts."
— BERTRAND RUSSELL

"We take what we know a little too seriously."
— NASSIM TALEB

"There's always a bigger junkyard dog."
— DENNIS GARTMAN

"The graveyards of Wall Street are filled with
those who thought they could do no wrong."
— MARK HULBERT

Money Managers

"I manage the fund as if
it was my own money."
— GEORGE SOROS

"In this business [money management],
if you are good, you're right
six times out of ten."
— PETER LYNCH

"No one takes care of a ship
like those who sail it."
— THOMAS S. MONSON

"Trust everyone, but cut the cards."
(use an independent auditor/banker)

"Investigate before you invest."
— WILLIAM ARTHUR WARD (1921-1994)
author and educator,
and CHARLES MERRILL (Merrill Lynch)

"A blindfolded monkey throwing darts at
a newspaper's financial pages could select a
portfolio that would be do just as well as one
carefully selected by the experts."
— BURT MALKIEL, *A Random Walk Down Wall Street*

"Professional investing has become
a loser's game. Individual investors investing
on their own do even worse —
on average, much worse."
— CHARLES ELLIS
Winning the Loser's Game

"The Rothschilds have no friends,
only clients."
— OLD FRENCH SAYING

"Nobody spends somebody else's money as
carefully as he spends his own."
— MILTON FRIEDMAN

"Why is an investment banker like a bird dog?
Because he will hunt with anyone who has a gun."
— JOHN WHITNEY

"The mutual fund industry is one place
where you never get what you pay for.
You get precisely what you don't pay for.
So if you pay nothing, you get everything."
— JACK BOGLE

"To be successful in business and investing, you've got to have skin in the game, a stake in the company."
— WARREN BUFFETT

"Even the best hitters in baseball have slumps."
— MARK SKOUSEN

"Beware of portfolio managers who are worried about their legacy."
— BILL HENRY

"The biggest problem with a famous money manager is an obsessive ego trip."
— LARRY TISCH

"I'm a money manager. I manage your money until it's all gone."
— WOODY ALLEN

"Your biggest tool when dealing with investments managed by someone else is . . . prayer."
— HARRY NEWTON

Other People's Money

"The key to financial success
and building wealth is to use OPM –
Other People's Money."
— MILLIONAIRE SPECULATOR

"The problem is that pretty soon
you run out of other people's money."
— MARGARET THATCHER

Getting Taken, Financial Frauds

"Nobody is immune to sucker bets."
— EDWIN LEFEVRE

"Avoid the promoter, the 'penny share,'
the new stock with a glamour or romance
title, the 'boiler room' operator
and 'sucker list' mailings."
— GERALD LOEB

"No warning can save a people determined
to grow suddenly rich."*
— LORD OVERSTONE

"Some stockbrokers make money the
old-fashioned way: They churn it."
— DAN DORFMAN

"There is never just one cockroach."
— DENNIS GARTMAN

"You can't shine a sneaker."
— GARY LAPIERRE (Boston WBZ Radio)

"That's blue sky."

Most analysts attribute the term "blue sl to a former Supreme Court Justice who wrote about companies selling stock which was not worth much more than a 'patch of blue sky,' but unfortunately no one has been able to produce a court decision with this statement in it. Others suggest that these laws protect people from companies who claim "nothing but blue sky" in their future, implying that they are sound, safe, and secure investments.

Investing

buys or sells against
bler is a man who
market."
— Jesse Livermore

f the market place
should be translated, Gambler, beware."
— Nicholas Darvas
Wall Street: The Other Las Vegas

"Wall Street is a gambling house peopled with
dealers, croupiers and touts on one side, and
with winners and suckers on the other."
— Nicholas Darvas

"I was no longer betting blindly, but earnings
my successes by hard study and clear thinking.
My great discovery was that a man must study
general conditions, to size them so as to be
able to anticipate probabilities."
— Jesse Livermore

"Never leave to chance what you
can achieve through calculation."
— Cardinal Richelieu

"Better to be lucky than smart."
— UNKNOWN

"A blind groundhog can
occasionally find an acorn."
— UNKNOWN

"The greatest lesson in life is to know that
even fools are right some times."
— WINSTON CHURCHILL

"Gambling: The sure way of getting
nothing for something."*
— WILSON MIZNER

"I'm a great believer in luck, and I find the
harder I work the more I have of it."
— THOMAS JEFFERSON

"Someday my boat will come in —
and with my luck I'll be at the airport."
— GRAFFITO

"Luck trumps skill in the short run."
— ASMATH DAMODARAN

"Chance favors only the mind
that is prepared."
— LOUIS PASTEUR

Fools and Their Money

"A fool and his money are soon parted."
— BEN FRANKLIN

"What I want to know is how they got
together in the first place."
— CYRIL FLETCHER

"There was a time when a fool
and his money were soon parted,
but now it happens to everybody."
— ADLAI STEVENSON

———

Financial Privacy
and Low Profile

"I don't own big hats,
but I have a lot of cattle."
— TEXAS MILLIONAIRE

"Let everyone know thee,
but let no man know thee thoroughly."
— BEN FRANKLIN

"The right most valued by all civilized men is
the right to be left alone."
— SUPREME COURT JUSTICE LOUIS D. BRANDEIS

"There was an old chap who never
volunteered advice and never bragged of his
winnings. If he went wrong he never whined.
The old jigger was rich."
— EDWIN LEFEVRE

"Keep your head below the trenches."
— FRANK BLISS'S FAVORITE MOTTO

"Plenty happens in Wall Street that no one
ever knows about."
— EARL SPARLING
Mystery Men of Wall Street

"The vast majority of people
dislike to be alone."
— HUMPHREY NEILL

"Keep quiet and speculate."
— GEORGE SOROS

Independent Thinking

"Good investment ideas are rare, valuable, and
subject to appropriation just as good product
or acquisition ideas are."
— WARREN BUFFETT

"My idea of a group decision
is to look in the mirror."
— WARREN BUFFETT

"A lone amateur built the ark; a large group
of professionals built the Titanic."
— UNKNOWN

"Nothing is more frustrating to an
individualist than to be mired in a modern
group-led, massive, corporate organization."
— HUMPHREY NEILL

"On a sled every dog save the lead dog
has the same view."
— DICK HECKMANN

Honesty and Integrity in Investing

"I need money, badly, but not badly enough
to do one dishonorable, shady, borderline,
or 'fast' thing to get it."
— ERNEST HEMINGWAY

"When you're rich,
you can afford to be honest."
— MARK SKOUSEN

"A clear conscience is nothing
but a poor memory."
— RICK RULE

Market Psychology

"Psychology is probably the most important factor in the market – and one that is least understood."
— DAVID DREMAN

"I can calculate the motion of heavenly bodies, but not the madness of people."
— SIR ISAAC NEWTON

"Nothing is more suicidal than a rational investment policy in an irrational world."
— JOHN MAYNARD KEYNES

Thinking vs. Feeling

"Don't think, feel!"
— BRUCE LEE

"Don't feel, think!"
— AYN RAND

"Don't think, look!"
— JIM DINES

"It isn't the head but the stomach that
determines the fate of the stock picker."
— PETER LYNCH

"Emotions are your worst enemy
in the stock market."
— DON HAYS
stock market commentator

"Profits should be based not on optimism
but on arithmetic."
— BEN GRAHAM

"Math wins."
— JIM BOWEN

Value vs. Price

"Know value, not prices."
— ARNOLD BERNHARD
founder, Value Line

"A critic is someone who knows the price
of everything, and the value of nothing."
— OSCAR WILDE

"Price is what you pay. Value is what you get."
— WARREN BUFFETT

"To know values is to know
the meaning of the market."
— CHARLES DOW

"Successful investing is anticipating
the anticipations of others."
— JOHN MAYNARD KEYNES

"In the short term, the market is
a voting machine.
In the long run, it is a weighing machine."
— BEN GRAHAM

"Investing is an activity of forecasting
the yield over the life of the asset;
speculation is the activity of forecasting
the psychology of the market."
— JOHN MAYNARD KEYNES

"The market takes no prisoners."
— ANONYMOUS

"The market is like a beautiful woman —
endlessly fascinating, endlessly complex,
always changing, always mystifying."
— EDWARD C. JOHNSON
Fidelity Management

"The stock market is like a wife —
when you come home, you never know
if you are going to be greeted with a kiss,
or hit with a frying pan."
— C. VERN MYERS

"It's not the strongest of the species that
survive, nor the most intelligent,
but the one most responsive to change."
— CHARLES DARWIN

"You don't get what you want from investing,
you get what you deserve."
— BILL BONNER

A Rich Man's Pearl of Wisdom #2
"Two Little Words."

When I was a young man, I had the opportunity to meet one of Wall Street's legends, Arnold Bernhard, founder of the Value Line Investment Survey, called "the most trusted name in investment research." Bernhard pioneered Value Line, famous for its one-page assessment of publicly-traded companies.

We had lunch together at his offices on 3rd Avenue in mid-Manhattan, and I shall never forget the occasion. He was in his late eighties by then and had only a year or two to live.

Bernhard wanted to talk about his offshore properties in the Bahamas (I lived in Nassau for two years, 1984-85), but I had a more philosophical interest.

I asked, "Mr. Bernhard, you have lived a long, successful career on Wall Street. If you could reduce your approach to investing to one sentence, what would it be?"

He reached for his cane, stood up, and walked slowly toward the window overlooking 42nd Street. "Young man," he said deliberately, "the secret to successful investing can be reduce to two simple words: *know value.*"

He said that everyone on Wall Street knew the prices of stocks and other assets, but few understood what these assets were really worth, or what they would be worth in the future. Paraphrasing Oscar Wilde, Bernhard declared, "Brokers, security analysts and investors — the whole lot — know the price of everything and the value of nothing."

According to Bernhard, investors have no sense of history. They know little about what makes markets move and are only successful as long as the trend doesn't change. But what happens when the trend changes and a bull market turns into a treacherous bear market, or vice versa? "Then people find out what real values are!" concluded Bernhard.

Bulls and Bears

"Bears make headlines, bulls make money."*

"Bulls never sleep." (always optimistic)

"Nobody is more bearish
than a sold-out bull."*

"There's no bear like a late bear."

"There is no bull like a licked bear."

"No price is too low for a bear
or too high for a bull."
— OLD PROVERB ON WALL STREET

"There's only one side to the stock market;
it is not the bull side or the bear side,
but the right side."
— JESSE LIVERMORE

"A bull market bails you out
of all your mistakes.
Bear markets make you pay
for your mistakes."
— DICK RUSSELL

"Better to be out of a bull market
than fully invested in a bear market."
— BILL HENRY

"You make your money from bad times
and collect your money in good times."
— ARTHUR B. LAFFER

Bull Markets

"A bull market doesn't like company."
— ANONYMOUS

"A bull market lasts until it's over."
— JIM DINES

"A trend is motion stays in motion,
until it stops."
— JIM DINES

"All bull markets end badly."
— BEN GRAHAM

"Bull markets die with a whimper,
not with a bang."
— UNKNOWN

"Don't confuse brains with a bull market."
— HUMPHREY B. NEILL

"A rising tide lifts all boats."
— OLD WALL STREET SLOGAN

"Most bull markets have a copper ceiling."
— ANTHONY M. GALLEA

"There's always a bull market somewhere."
— ROBERT KINSMAN

"This country is very elastic . . .
like a rubber ball hit,
it will spring up again."
— WILLIAM VANDERBILT

"Nothing is more difficult than
holding on to your stocks in a bull market."
— JIM DINES

"The next 100% in the market will be up,
not down."
— SCOTT R. MATTHEWS

Bear Markets

"In a bear market, the man who wins
is the man who loses the least."
— DICK RUSSELL

"A bear market returns capital to
those who it rightly belongs to."
— IAN MCAVITY

"Markets that will not go down
on bearish news are not bear markets."
— DENNIS GARTMAN

"If you are a long-term investor,
you will view a bear market
as an opportunity to make money."
— JOHN TEMPLETON

"Bear markets usually end not with a bang
but a whimper."
— RICHARD BAND

"When the paddy wagon rolls up, they take away the good girls with the bad."
— OLD WALL STREET SAYING

"When falling, dive."
— JIM DINES

"A bear market descends a slope of hope."
— ROBERT PRECHTER

"The end is not nigh: people and markets adapt to even the worst circumstances."
— DAVID TEPPER

Doomsdayers and Cassandras

"Everything will end badly."
— BILL HENRY

"It wasn't raining when Noah built the ark."
— HOWARD RUFF

"A stopped watch is right twice a day."
— ANONYMOUS

"Businessmen can profit handsomely
if they will disregard the pessimistic auguries
of self-appointed prophets of doom."
— J. PAUL GETTY

"Many an optimist has become rich
simply by buying out a pessimist."
— LAURENCE J. PETER

"The man who is a bear on the United States
will eventually go broke."
— J. P. MORGAN

"Unless you are a short seller,
it never pays to be pessimistic."
— PETER LYNCH

Panics and Crashes

"Never underestimate the size of a panic,
nor the power of the politician."
— HARRY D. SCHULTZ

"Trying to pick the bottom in a crash
is like catching a falling knife."
— ANONYMOUS

"Owners of sound securities
should never panic."
— J. PAUL GETTY

The Crash of 1929

Merryle Rukeyser, Louis Rukeyser's father, happened to encounter Bernard Baruch on the street when the stock market crashed in 1929. "This is a terrible day in the stock market," said Mr. Rukeyser. "Not for buyers," answered Mr. Baruch.

Technical and Cycle Analysis

"History repeats itself
all the time on Wall Street."
— EDWIN LEFEVRE

"History may not repeat itself,
but it rhymes."
— MARK TWAIN

"History repeats itself,
but never in the same way."
— MARK SKOUSEN

"I know of no way of judging
the future but by the past."
— PATRICK HENRY

"Dip in the morning, sellers take warning."
— OLD WALL STREET SAW

"Sell in May and go away."
— OLD WALL STREET SAYING

"Never short a dull market."
— OLD TRADER'S ADAGE

"The trend is your friend."

"Go with the flow.
Make the trend your friend."
— ANONYMOUS

"The trend is your friend, until it ends."
— JIM DINES

"The trendless market is friendless to traders."
— HUMPHREY NEILL

"Never bet against the market."
— MICHAEL MASTERSON

"It's easier to row a boat
downriver than upriver."
— JIM DINES

"No stock goes in a straight line."
— ANTHONY M. GALLEA

"There's nothing wrong with the charts,
only the chartists."
— OLD TRADER'S REFRAIN

"The longer the base, the higher the space."
— TECHNICAL TRADER

Technical Charting: Pro and Con

"What do interest rates have to do with the market? Nothing. What does inflation have to do with the market? Nothing. What do OPEC prices have to do with the market? Nothing. What does war have to do with the market? Nothinnnnggg!"
— Joe Granville
Technical Trader

"I realized that technical analysis didn't work when I turned the chart upside-down and didn't get a different answer."
— Warren Buffett

"Heavy volume, price rises —
light volume, price falls."
— Michael D. Sheimo

"Prices have no memory."
— Anonymous

"Facts are history."
— Unknown

"Everything eventually reverts to the mean."
— Frank Holmes

Fundamental Analysis

"You must be a fundamentalist to be
really successful in the market."
— JOHN TEMPLETON

"If you like the story, buy the stock."
— PETER LYNCH

"Technicians look ahead,
fundamentalists look backwards.
The true language of the market is technical."
— JOE GRANVILLE

"Buying stocks without studying the
companies is the same as playing poker
and never looking at your cards."
— PETER LYNCH

"Games are won by players who focus on the
playing field, not by those whose eyes
are glued to the scoreboard."
— WARREN BUFFETT

To Buy or Not to Buy: Two Views

"The only sound reason for my buying a stock
is that it is rising in price."
— NICHOLAS DARVAS

"The dumbest reason in the world
to buy a stock is because it's going up."
— WARREN BUFFETT

Education and Experience

"The used key is always bright."
— BEN FRANKLIN

"In my whole life, I have known no
wise people who didn't read all the time
— none, zero."
— CHARLIE MUNGER

"Nothing grows in the shadow of an oak tree."
— T. ROWE PRICE

"Genius without education is like
silver in the mine."
— BEN FRANKLIN

"Experience keeps a dear school,
yet fools will learn in no other."
— BEN FRANKLIN

"The best way to learn how to invest
is to invest."
— HUGO KOEHLER

"Some of the most successful investors I know
have no technique that can be defined,
beyond knowledge, realism, and industry:
no theory, no generalizations."
— JOHN TRAIN
The Money Masters

"A man who goes hunting once a year
rarely comes home with game."
— JULIAN M. SNYDER

"If you don't know who you are, the stock
market is an expensive place to find out."
— GEORGE GOODMAN

"Money talks, bullsh*t walks."
— WALL STREET LINE

"There are old traders and bold traders,
but there aren't any old, bold traders."
— ANTHONY M. GALLEA

"The stock market is a place where
a man with experience gains money and
a man with money gains some experience."*
— DANIEL DREW

"He who refuses to study history
has no past and no future."
— ROBERT HEINLEIN

"We learn from history that
we do not learn from history."
— HEGEL

"The price of education is paid only once.
The cost of ignorance must be paid forever."
— TED NICHOLAS

"You have to study a great deal
to learn a little."
— MONTESQUIEU

"A page of history is worth a volume of logic."
— OLIVER WENDELL HOLMES

"Much learning does not teach wisdom."
— HERACLITUS OF EPHESUS

"If all men profited by experience, the world
would be peopled exclusively by the wise."
— EDWIN LEFEVRE

"Only when the tide goes out do you
discover who's been swimming naked."*
— WARREN BUFFETT

"Knowledge is about the past;
investment is about the future."
— GEORGE GILDER

"An investment in knowledge
pays the best interest."
— BEN FRANKLIN

"If you don't know history, you're history."
— MARK SKOUSEN

"The father buys, the son builds,
the grandson sells, and his son begs."
— OLD ENGLISH PROVERB

"Every person has a plan until he gets
punched in the mouth."
— MIKE TYSON

The Story of Trading Sardines

There's an old story about three commodity traders who were into the sardines market. The first trader bought a thousand cans of sardines for $6 per can and soon had them sold to the second trader for $12 per can. The second trader passed them along to the third trader for $24 per can. The third trader figured that if the market for sardines collapsed, he could at least eat them.

Finally, the market did collapse, and the last owner decided to open a can and eat some sardines. But he was startled to discover that the sardines were rancid. He went back to the second trader and demanded his money back. "These sardines are no good," he exclaimed.

"Of course, they're no good," replied the dealer. "Those sardines are not for eating — they're trading sardines!"

— Story told by Doug Casey

"When history repeats itself,
the price goes up."

"It is better to learn by knowledge
than by experience."

In times of rapid change,
experience could be your worst enemy.
— J. PAUL GETTY

"If past history was all there is to the
[investment] game, the richest people
would be librarians."
— WARREN BUFFETT

"You have to get the facts first,
then you have to face the facts."
— PAUL CABOT

"The four most dangerous words in the world
of investing are: This time is different."
— JOHN TEMPLETON

"The further back you look, the further
forward you can see."
— WINSTON CHURCHILL

"If you don't use your head,
you'll use your feet."
— JIM DINES

"Go for a business that any idiot can run—
because sooner or later, any idiot
is probably going to run it."
— PETER LYNCH

"If we are in a transition period, the person in
the most danger is the one who has recently
done well, because he's done well on things
that are about to change."
— DEAN LeBARON
(Battlemarch Financial Management)

"The stock market takes the stairs up,
and the elevator down."
— OLD WALL STREET SAYING

Rules of Investing

"You must devote some time every day
to the subject of investment."
— GERALD LOEB

"My first rule is to buy only
something that is quoted daily."
— GERALD LOEB

"If a stock doesn't act right, don't touch it."
— EDWIN LEFEVRE

"When in doubt, stay out."
— JIM DINES

"Haste makes waste."
— BEN FRANKLIN

"Patience in market is worth
pounds in a year."
— BEN FRANKLIN

"If you are going to panic, panic early."
— JESSE LIVERMORE

"When a friend deals with a friend, let the bargain be clear and well penned, that they may continue friends to the end."
— BEN FRANKLIN

"There's a million stories in the Naked City."
— WALL STREET ADAGE

"Look at investments coldly, allowing no sentiment to play any part."
— GERALD LOEB

"Cut short your losses, and let your profits run."
— DAVID RICARDO'S
golden rule of investing
(later attributed to Daniel Drew)

"Better to buy part of a company than the whole company."
— WARREN BUFFETT

"Never buy a stock immediately after
a substantial rise or sell one
immediately after a substantial fall."
— BEN GRAHAM

"Sell the losers and let the winners run."
— MICHAEL D. SHEIMO

"Don't prune your flowers
and water your weeds."
— ANTHONY M. GALLEA

"Better to preserve capital on the downside
than outperform the market on the upside."
— WILLIAM J. LIPPMAN

"Should you find yourself in a chronically
leaking boat, energy devoted to changing
vessels is likely to be more productive than
energy devoted to patching leaks."
— WARREN BUFFETT

"Marry a wife, not a stock."
— ANONYMOUS

"It's easy to get married in a bull market."
— Unknown

"Don't let a stock go stale on you."
— Jesse Livermore

"Always sell half on a double."
— Yale Hirsch

"Do not trade during times of personal stress."
— Horace E. Sense

"If you can keep your head when all about
you are losing theirs."
— Rudyard Kipling

"A good speculation should be a good
investment."
— Old saying on Wall Street

"When Santa doesn't call, beware."
— Yale Hirsch
(bear markets usually follow
if stocks don't rally in December)

"Buy on Monday, sell on Friday."
— YALE HIRSCH
author, *Never Sell Stocks on Monday.*

"If a stock goes down five days in a row,
sell it."
— ACE GREENBERG

"You make money watching."
— CHICAGO COMMODITY TRADER

"Money follows earnings."
— DAVID DREMAN

"Don't fight the tape."
Or "Don't argue with the tape."
— EDWIN LEFEVRE

"Don't follow the crowd, learn the tape!"
— HUMPHREY NEILL

"Well bought is half sold."
— ANONYMOUS

"Have the best hand, the best draw,
or get out."
— OLD WEST SAYING

"Cutting losses is the one and only rule
of the markets."
— GERALD LOEB

"It's better to average up than down."
— MICHAEL D. SHEIMO

"When there's nothing to do, do nothing."
— LARRY TISCH

"Think global, stay local."
— TOM HUDSON

"The worst mistake is taking profits too soon,
and losses too long."
— MICHAEL PRICE

"When in doubt, get out."
— OLD WALL STREET ADAGE

"Own more of what's working
and less of what's not."
— DENNIS GARTMAN

"Never tell them what you're going to do
until you done it."
— COMMODORE VANDERBILT

"Never buy what you don't want
or sell what you ain't got."
— COMMODORE VANDERBILT

Long-term Investing vs. Short-Term Speculating

"Speculating is an effort,
probably unsuccessful, to turn a little money
into a lot. Investment is an effort,
which should be successful, to prevent
a lot of money from becoming a little."
— FRED SCHWED, JR.

"A shareholder not selling is as good as
somebody else buying."

"More money is made in the stock market
when you buy than when you sell."

"Money is made by sitting, not trading."
— JESSE LIVERMORE

"It never was my thinking that made the big
money for me. It always was sitting."
— EDWIN LEFEVRE

"Buy right, sit tight."
— JESSE LIVERMORE

"Plant the tree, and let it grow."
— T. ROWE PRICE

"Do not be in a hurry to take a profit."
— JESSE LIVERMORE

"Moves almost always
take longer than expected."
— JIM DINES

"Men who can both be right
and sit tight are uncommon."
— EDWIN LEFEVRE

"To be successful, you need leisure."
— GEORGE SOROS

"Aimless switching gathers no profits."
— HUMPHREY NEILL

"Turnover is vanity; profit is sanity."
— CATWG THE WISE
(Welch)

"Traders come and go;
risk managers are here to stay."
— NASSIM TALEB

"It's easier to buy than to sell."
— UNKNOWN

"Better to get a fast nickel than a slow dime."
— BOB ALLEN

"It take time to make money."
— JESSE LIVERMORE

"Don't give me timing.
Give me time."
— JESSE LIVERMORE

"Nobody can catch all the fluctuations."
— EDWIN LEFEVRE

"I never attempt to make money on the stock
market. I buy on the assumption that they
could close the market the next day
and not reopen it for five years."
— WARREN BUFFETT

"The best way to put odds in your favor is to invest long-term."
— DICK DAVIS

"Everyone is a disciplined, long-term investor until the market goes down."
— STEVE FORBES

"Bank on the trends and don't worry about the tremors."
— J. PAUL GETTY

"Don't do something, just stand there."
— JACK BOGLE
(advice during a crisis)

"Time is your friend; impulse is your enemy."
— JACK BOGLE

"The big profits go to the intelligent, careful and patient investor, not to the reckless and overeager speculator."
— J. PAUL GETTY
How to Be Rich

"Conservative investors sleep well."
— title of a book by
PHILIP FISHER

"Investing is the greatest game in the world.
It's like baseball except that you
never have to swing.
All day you wait for the pitch you like;
then when the fielders are asleep,
you step up and hit it."
— WARREN BUFFETT

"Day trading is a sucker's game.
Don't do it—ever."
— CHARLES ELLIS

"Investors make more money with the seats of
their pants than the soles of their feet."
— LUCIEN O. HOOPER,
Forbes columnist 1949-1979

"There are two times in a man's life
when he should not speculate:
when he can't afford to and when he can."
— MARK TWAIN

Value vs. Growth

"Value outperforms growth
about 70% of the time.
The investing tortoise
beats the speculative hare."
— DAVID DREMAN

"Avoid the growth trap:
the most innovative companies
are rarely the best place for investors."
— JEREMY SIEGEL

"Obvious prospects for growth
in a business do not translate into
obvious profits for investors."
— BENJAMIN GRAHAM

"Value investors make the mistake
of buying too soon and selling too soon.
Growth investors make the mistake
of buying too late and selling too late."
— WARREN BOROSON

Large Cap vs. Small Cap

"Who says elephants can't dance?"
— Louis V. Gerstner, Jr.
(former CEO, IBM)

"If you have large cap, mid cap and small cap,
and the market declines,
you're going to have less cap."
— Martin Truax

Personal Philosophy

"The door to the American Millionaire's Club
is not locked."
— J. PAUL GETTY

"There is only one success — to be able to
spend your life in your own way."
— CHRISTOPHER MORLEY

"Great almsgiving lessens no man's living."
— BEN FRANKLIN

"What's the best investment I ever made?
Charity. I never lost a dime."
— JOHN TEMPLETON

"The best investment advice you can ever give
or receive is 'Stay healthy.'"
— *DICK DAVIS DIVIDEND*

"Half wits talk much and say little."
— BEN FRANKLIN

"There is no error so monstrous that it fails to find defenders among the ablest men."
— LORD ACTON

"Make yourself a sheep, and you'll find a wolf nearby."*
— OLD RUSSIAN PROVERB

"There is no great genius without some touch of madness."
— SENECA

"Nothing can prevent some seats in the theater from being better than others."
— CHRYSIPPUS

"The great thing in this world is not so much where we stand, as in what direction we are moving."
— OLIVER WENDELL HOLMES

"There is no greater obstacle to learning than to be the prisoner of totally invalid but dogmatic theories."
— PETER F. DRUCKER

"All wars are the results of undefended wealth."
— Douglas MacArthur

"When it comes to money,
we all have the same religion."
— Voltaire

"If you're not healthy, you're not wealthy."
— R. E. McMaster

"The successful man is not so superior
in ability as in action."
— Roger Babson

"We are all ignorant, just in different things."
— Hugh Nibley

"There is nothing more terrible
than ignorance in action."
— Goethe

"Life is a journey, not a destination."
— Anonymous

"A man with money is no match
against a man on a mission."
— Ziad K. Abdelnour

"It is the irritation of the oyster
that forms the pearl."
— ANONYMOUS

"Superior people never make long visits."
— ANONYMOUS

"If I have been able to see farther than others,
it was because I stood
on the shoulder of giants."
— ISAAC NEWTON

"The only people who never get criticized
are those who never do anything."
— LINDA PREVATT

"Science progresses one funeral at a time."
— MAX PLANCK

"I've known people who have
turned down money, but never respect."
— GREEK SAYING

"You should give your kids enough money to
do anything
but not enough money to do nothing."
— WARREN BUFFETT

"If you don't drive your business,
you will be driven out of business."
— FRANK HOLMES

"Remember, there are men
behind each stock."
— JESSE LIVERMORE

"If you want to make money,
go where the money is."
— EUGENE JACKSON'S FATHER

"Nothing but money is sweeter than honey."
— BEN FRANKLIN

"Money may build you a house,
but not a home."
— MARK SKOUSEN

Taxes and Investing

"There's nothing sinister in so arranging one's
affairs as to keep taxes as low as possible."
— JUDGE LEARNED HAND

"Better to take your chances on a tax shelter
than giving it to the government."
— LARRY ABRAHAM

"There would be no tax havens
without tax hells."
— OLD SWISS BANKER SAYING

"Nobody gets rich taking tax deductions."
— ANONYMOUS

"Never let taxes get in the way of profits."
— ANONYMOUS

"What does it profit a person to gain a tax
break when he loses his principal?"
— ANONYMOUS

"You don't lose money to make money."
— ANONYMOUS

"Trying to minimize taxes too much
is one of the great causes of
really dumb mistakes in investing."
— CHARLIE MUNGER

"One correct move is far better than
all the tax savings you can do in a lifetime."
— VINOD KHOSLA
co-founder of Sun Microsystems

Government and Wall Street

"Bad government drives out good business."
— MARK SKOUSEN

"Capitalism without failure
is like religion without hell."
— CHARLIE MUNGER

"No man's life, liberty, or property are safe
while the legislature is in session."
— JUDGE GIDEON TUCKER
(1866)

"Being the richest man on a sinking ship
is a bitter victory."
— JOHN A. PUGSLEY

"Successful preservation of capital
must overcome the handicaps of socialistic
governments, supposedly to help the masses."
— GERALD LOEB

"The ultimate result of protecting fools from their folly is to fill the planet full of fools."
— SIR JAMES RUSSELL LOWELL

"Avoid investing in those countries with a high level of socialist or government regulation of business. Business growth depends on a strong free-enterprise system."
— JOHN TEMPLETON

"The king reigns, but the banker rules."
— JACOB FUGGER

"Don't fight the Fed — fear the Fed."
— MICHAEL SINCERE,
MarketWatch

"There have been three great inventions since the beginning of time:
The fire, the wheel, and central banking."
— WILL ROGERS

"Get your money out of the country before the country gets the money out of you."
— HARRY BROWNE

"When the King is far the people are happy."
— CHINESE PROVERB

"When Washington sleeps,
the economy grows."
— WILLIAM REES-MOGG

"What is the greatest danger to your
investments? Inflation."
— PAUL CABOT

"If printing money helped the economy,
then counterfeiting should be legal."
— BRIAN WESBURY

"The government cannot guarantee against
losses. The public must be its own watch dog.
Look within yourself, and then, Mister Trader,
you won't have to look out."
— EDWIN LEFEVRE

"War is always bearish on money —
and a good time to buy."
— PHILIP FISHER

"Where stands our total freedom in the
absence of financial freedom?"
— ROBERT KINSMAN

The Value of the Dollar and Currencies

"At its creation the only destiny
a currency has is devaluation."
— DR. FRANZ PICK

"Government is the only agency that can take
a valuable commodity like paper, slap some
ink on it, and make it totally worthless."*
— LUDWIG VON MISES

"Inflation: When nobody has enough money
because everybody has too much."
— HAROLD COFFIN

Investing in Gold

"He who owns the gold, makes the rules."
— OLD GOLD BUG SAYING

"Without gold, we fold."
— SLOGAN, AMERICAN GOLD NEWS

"All that glitters isn't gold,
but the really good stuff is."
— CHIP WOOD

"The desire for gold is the most universal
and deeply rooted commercial instinct
of the human race."
— GERALD LOEB
The Battle for Investment Survival

"Most brokers don't know
a mine from a pinecone."
— SAM PARKS

"You can't print wealth,
you must produce it."
— KENNETH J. GERBINO

"You have to sift through a lot of dirt
before you find gold."
— UNKNOWN

"The impact of the rate of inflation
on the price of gold is like
tracking the footprints of an animal."
— JULIAN M. SNYDER

"I collect businesses and friends, not gold."
— WARREN BUFFETT

"Gold is the hitching post
of the monetary universe."
— JIM DINES

"The only currency still used as a
store of value after 5,000 years is gold."
— MARTIN TRUAX

"Every piece of gold jewelry or coin ever made
still has value. Can you say the same thing
about stocks or bonds?"
— NICHOLAS COLAS

Penny Stocks and Gold Bugs

"When the wind blows,
even the turkeys will fly."

— JERRY POGUE

"Most penny stocks are like burning matches.
If you hold them long enough,
you get burned."

— JEFF PHILLIPS

"In the beginning the promoter has the
dream, and the public has the money . . .
My job is to arrange a transfer."

— VANCOUVER PROMOTER

"Cancel the public offering. We found gold!"

— famous line from a
penny mining stock promoter

"Own enough to make a difference."

— ROBERT BISHOP

"What's the definition of a gold mine?
A hole in the ground surrounded by a liar."

— MARK TWAIN

"In Canada, they don't even have the hole."

— STEVE SAKER

Wall Street vs. Main Street

"Wall Street exaggerates everything."
— MARK SKOUSEN

"The business of investing is not the same as investing in a business."
— MARK SKOUSEN
Investing in One Lesson (2007)

"The stock market and the economy are two different things."
— MILTON FRIEDMAN

"I buy companies, not stocks."
— WARREN BUFFETT

"Good CEOs know everything about their company and little about their stock."
— *DICK DAVIS DIVIDEND*

"Money won is twice as sweet
as money earned."
— FAST EDDIE FELSON
(Paul Newman in "The Color of Money")

"Good companies may not be
good investments."
— ASMATH DAMODARAN

"If a business does well,
the stock eventually follows."
— WARREN BUFFETT

"Although it's easy to forget sometimes,
a share of stock is not a lottery ticket.
It's part ownership of a business."
— PETER LYNCH
One Up on Wall Street

"Do you want to be right about the economy
or make money?"
— question by broker to an economist
(from DENNIS SLOTHOWER)

"The stock market seldom has a normal day."
— MICHAEL D. SHEIMO

"Why is it that some of the most
successful people in business and life
can be utter failures in the stock market?"
— MARK SKOUSEN

"Wall Street and Main Street are like a
rocky marriage with frequent separations,
but never a divorce."
— MARK SKOUSEN

"Investment is most intelligent
when it is most businesslike."
— WARREN BUFFETT

"The market can stay irrational
longer than you can stay solvent."
— JOHN MAYNARD KEYNES

"No news is bad news on Wall Street."
— MARK SKOUSEN

Diversification vs. Concentration

"It's not a stock market,
it's a market of stocks."
— OLD WALL STREET ADAGE

"Stretch your feet according to the blanket."
— KURDISH PROVERB

"The really great fortunes were made by
concentration, not diversification."
— GERALD LOEB
The Battle for Investment Survival

"To make it, concentrate;
to keep it, diversify."
— MARK SKOUSEN

"I'm no genius.
I'm smart in spots,
and I stay around those spots."
— THOMAS WATSON, SR.

"A man's got to know his limitations."
— HARRY CALLAHAN
(Clint Eastwood in "Dirty Harry")

"Over diversification is a poor protection
against lack of knowledge."
— GERALD LOEB

"I believe in pyramiding, not averaging."
— GERALD LOEB

"If you have a little, use a rifle.
If you have a lot, use a shotgun."
— ANONYMOUS

"Don't struggle to find the needle in the
haystack; just buy the haystack."
— JACK BOGLE

"Owning stock is like having children. Don't
get involved with more than you can handle."
— PETER LYNCH

"Eggs in One Basket": Diversify or Concentrate?

"Don't put all your eggs in one basket."
— OLD BANKER LINE

Put all your eggs in one basket,
and watch that basket.
— MARK TWAIN
(Samuel Langhorne Clemens) [1835-1910]
used the phrase in *Pudd'nhead Wilson*, Chapter 15.
Quoted by Andrew Carnegie in
"How to Succeed in Life," 1903.

"Forget the eggs, enjoy the omelet."
— ANONYMOUS

"Money is like manure. You have to spread it
around to make things grow."
— J. PAUL GETTY

"I'd rather win one big tournament in my
entire life than make the cut every week."
— ARNOLD PALMER

"Buy two of everything in sight and you end
up with a zoo instead of a portfolio."
— WARREN BUFFETT

"A jack of all trades will never be rich."
— ADAM SMITH
Wealth of Nations (1776)

"Be a hedge hog, not a fox.
The fox knows many little things,
but the hedge hog knows one big thing."
— JOHN TRAIN

"It is easier to follow a few stocks well
than it is to follow a well full of stocks."
— S. A. NELSON
The ABC of Stock Speculation

Losing Money in the Stock Market

"Investors are condemned almost by
mathematical law to lose."
— BENJAMIN GRAHAM
The Intelligent Investor

"I have always found it profitable
to study my mistakes."
— EDWIN LEFEVRE

"If you don't profit from your investment
mistakes, someone else will."
— YALE HIRSCH

"If you have trouble imaging a 20% loss in the
stock market, you shouldn't be in stocks."
— JACK BOGLE

"The first loss is the best."
— WALL STREET PROVERB

"The first loss is the smallest loss."
— ANTHONY M. GALLEA

"Happiness is good for the body, but it is grief which develops the strength of the mind."

— MARCEL PROUST

"There is nothing like losing all you have in the world for teaching you what not to do."

— EDWIN LEFEVRE

"Failure teaches success."

— JIM DAVIDSON

"Some people are never too old to find new ways to lose money."

— ANONYMOUS

"Bad news travels faster than good news."

— POOR RICHARD'S ALMANAC

"The men who try to do something and fail are infinitely better than those who try to do nothing and succeed."

— ANONYMOUS

"Don't ever try to learn from other people's
mistakes. Learn what other people do right."
— OLD RABBI SAYING

"Markets can remain irrational longer than
you can remain solvent."
— JOHN MAYNARD KEYNES

"But now I know
How rare a thing,
How truly rare
Is true despair!
— SAM HOFFENSTEIN (1930s)

"Laziness travels so slowly,
that poverty soon overtakes him."
— BEN FRANKLIN

"You learn only from your losses,
not your gains."
— ANONYMOUS

"After you buy a stock, it will go lower;
after you sell a stock, it will always go higher."
— DICK DAVIS

"Success can only be achieved
through repeated failure."
— SOICHIRO HONDA

"Money is easier lost than gained."

"The public is always wrong.
The market is always right."
— JESSE LIVERMORE

"The market will always tell you
when you are wrong."
— JESSE LIVERMORE

"Markets are never wrong — opinions are."
— JESSE LIVERMORE

"Don't make the same mistake once!"
(Similar to Warren Buffett's two rules of investing:
#1. Never lose money. #2. See rule #1.)

"When Buffett and Soros invest,
they're not focused on the profits
but on not losing money."
— MARK TIER

"Above all, avoid big mistakes."
— WARREN BUFFETT

"Charlie Munger and I have not learned how
to solve difficult business problems.
What we have learned is to avoid them."
— WARREN BUFFETT

"Don't throw good money after bad."
— UNKNOWN

"Never make a margin call."
— OLD RULE ON WALL STREET

"Profits always take care of themselves,
but losses never do."
— JESSE LIVERMORE

"Gravity works in the market as well as
science. It takes buying to move the market
up, but when buying dries up,
stocks will fall of their own weight."
— JESSE LIVERMORE

"Stocks decline much faster than they climb."
— JESSE LIVERMORE

"Those who always sell winners
and keep losers eventually accumulates
a portfolio of losers."

"Picking a winning stock is like
catching lightning in a bottle."

"Avoiding losers is every bit as important
as finding winners."
— ROGER MCNAMEE

"It's better to have 50% of something
than 100% of nothing."
— father of SUZE ORMAN

"A 50% loss requires a
100% gain to break even."
— BRIAN BERGHUTS
(T. Rowe Price)

"It's better to have seller's remorse than buyer's
remorse. If you have seller's remorse, you still
made money; if you have buyer's remorse,
it means you lost money for sure."
—RICH WHELAN, M. D.

"It is the mark of a great athlete to be bruised,
yet still conquer."
— ST. IGNATIUS OF ANTIOCH

Worrying about Losses

"The moving finger writes; and, having writ,
Moves on: nor all thy piety nor wit
Shall lure it back to cancel half a line,
Nor all thy tears wash out a word of it."
— RUBAIYAT OF OMAN KHAYYAM

"What man cannot reverse, he must endure."
— MEXICAN SAYING

"Accepting losses in the most important single
investment advice to insure safety of capital."
— GERALD LOEB

"A loss never bothers me after I take it."
— JESSE LIVERMORE

"Losses are a cost of doing business."
— JIM DINES

"You know who didn't have any bad years?
Bernie Madoff — until he got caught."
— KEN FISHER

When to Buy

"Now is always the most difficult
time to invest."
— ANONYMOUS

"Buy on the rumor, sell on the news."
— OLD SAYING ON WALL STREET

"The buyer needs a hundred eyes,
the seller not one."
— GEORGE HERBERT

"Well bought is half sold."
— ANONYMOUS

"One of the funny things about the stock
market is that every time one person buys,
another sells, and both think they are astute."
— WILLIAM FEATHER

"Buy good stocks at cheap prices
and hold on."
— DICK DAVIS

"The question of *when* to buy is far more
important than *what* to buy."
— ROGER W. BABSON

When to Sell

"Selling at the right time
is more difficult than buying."
— GERALD LOEB

"A good player knows when
to pick up his marbles."
— ANONYMOUS

"I know where I'm getting out before I get in."
— BRUCE KOVNER

Bernard Baruch:
Q. How can you sleep with all those
investments?

A. If any of them keep me awake, I sell them.

"Sell down to the sleeping point."
— BARNARD BARUCH

"Any fool can buy a stock.
It takes a smart investor
to know when to sell."
— ANONYMOUS

"Don't sell stocks when the sap
is running up the trees!"
— ADDISON CAMMACK, trader
(quoted in Edwin Lefevre)
Don't sell stocks when there's a bull market

"Stocks were made to be sold."
— GERALD LOEB

"When you feel like bragging,
it's probably time to sell."
— JOHN NEFF

Cutting Losses

"Cutting losses is the one and only rule
of the markets that can be taught."
— GERALD LOEB

"The odds are against a stock collapsing
and then coming back.
Take your loss and move on."
— DICK DAVIS

"A stop loss is a protection
from the black swan."
— NASSIM TALEB

"Always sit in an exit row."
— KEITH FITZ-GERALD

Taking Profits

"You never go broke taking a profit."
or "You never lose money by taking a profit."
— OLD SAYING ON WALL STREET

"They say you never grow poor taking profits,
but neither do you grow rich taking a
four-point profit in a bull market."
— EDWIN LEFEVRE

"When reward is at its pinnacle,
risk is near at hand."
— JACK BOGLE

"Feel the money in your fingers
once in a while."
— JESSE LIVERMORE

"Once you have achieved success,
reward yourself."
— JESSE LIVERMORE

"One profit in cash is worth two on paper."
— HUMPHREY NEILL

"Profits always take care of themselves
but losses never do."
— JESSE LIVERMORE

"Never let a profit turn into a loss."
— MARK SKOUSEN

"Don't let the perfect
be the enemy of the good."
— VOLTAIRE

Shorting the Market

"I was once advised to short a stock that inevitably was going to announce bad news. But I was reluctant to short it because we were in a strong bull market that was lifting all stocks, good and bad."
— UNKNOWN

"Never short a dull market."
— OLD WALL STREET ADAGE

"Never short the trend."
— MICHAEL D. SHEIMO

"If a stock is high enough to be sold, it is high enough to be sold short."
— RUSSELL SAGE

"It's easier to row down river than up river."
— JIM DINES

"Don't waste your time short-selling. Show me the short-sellers' yachts."
— RON BARON

"He who sells short...."

"Old Daniel Drew used to squeeze the boys
with some frequency and make them pay
high prices for the Erie 'sheers' they had sold
short to him. He was himself squeezed by
Commodore Vanderbilt in Erie,
and when old Drew begged for mercy the
Commodore grimly quoted the
Great Bear's own deathless distich:

"He who sells what isn't his'n
Must buy it back or go to pris'n."
— EDWIN LEFEVRE
Reminiscences of a Stock Operator

Fred Schwed Jr. in
Where are the Customers Yachts?,
added this ditty for buyers who can pay:

"He who buys what he can't pay for
Is not the man to shout 'Hooray' for."

Missed Investment Opportunities

For of all sad words of tongue or pen,
The saddest are these: It might have been!
— John Greenleaf Whittier

"A new train leaves the station
every ten minutes."
— Anonymous

"It's tough to catch the train
after it has left the station."
— Alexander Green

"The stock market is like a carousel,
you can get on or off the horses at any time."
— Ron Miller

"You can't kiss all the pretty girls."
— Anonymous

"To know, and not to act, is not to know."
— Wang Yank Ming (General, 880 AD),
quoted by Andrew Lanyi, broker

"You do not have to be fully invested
all the time."
— Gerald Loeb

"Sometimes the best investments
are the ones you don't make."
— Donald G. Smith

Formulas and Guaranteed Success

"Nothing is safe;
nothing is sure in any field of life."
— GERALD LOEB
The Battle for Investment Survival

"If there's anything I detest,
it's a mechanistic formula for anything.
People should use their heads and go by logic
and reason, not hard and fast rules."
— GERALD LOEB

"Any successful approach to investing
is bound to fail."
— WILSON'S RULE
(Robert Wilson)

"No trading system, no matter how good, will
work if too many people start following it."
— MARK HULBERT

"As people learn the old tricks,
new tricks have to be invented."
— GARET GARRETT

"No one can reduce speculation
to a single formula."
— MERRYLE RUKEYSER

"Past results are no guarantee of future
performance."
— CAVEAT ON TOMBSTONE SECURITIES AD

"In the business world, the rearview mirror is
always clearer than the windshield."
— WARREN BUFFETT

"Gather ye rosebuds while you may,
Old Time is still a-flying,
And this same flower that smiles today,
Tomorrow will be dying."
— ROBERT HERRICK
(1591-1674)

"If it's a sure deal, run."
— UNKNOWN

"Never forget: things change."
— LOWELL MILLER

"Mechanical forecasting will never
take the place of intelligent judgment."
— HUMPHREY NEILL

"The easiest way into Wall Street
is by the Hall of Delusions."
— GARET GARRETT

Bonds, Fixed Income, and Dividend-paying Stocks

"I don't know what the seven wonders
of the world are, but I know the eighth,
compound interest."
— BARON ROTHSCHILD

"One thousand dollars left to earn interest
at 8 per cent a year will grow to
$43 quadrillion in 400 years,
but the first hundred years are the hardest."
— SIDNEY HOMER

"Gentlemen prefer bonds."
— ANDREW MELLON
Businessman & financier (1855-1937)

"Bonds are guaranteed certificates
of confiscation."
— FRANZ PICK

"Earnings can lie, but dividends never do."
— GERALDINE WEISS
author, *Dividends Don't Lie*

"Dividends are the critical factor giving the
edge to most winning stocks in the long run."
— JEREMY SIEGEL

"A company can best serve its investors
by following a consistent,
predictable dividend policy."
— PHILIP FISHER

"Dividend growth is the true signal
of a prospering company."
— LOWELL MILLER
The Single Best Investment (2006)

"Cut the dividend, cut the loss."
— ANTHONY M. GALLEA

"If it's too good to believe,
it's going to be called."
— RICHARD LEHMANN

"Dividends are an outward sign
of inward grace."
— Douglas R. Casey

And renouncing illusions
Find peace and content
In that simplest sublimest of truths —
Six percent!
— Nicholas Biddle
(1886-1844)
President of 2nd Bank
of the United States

"Do you know the only thing
that gives me pleasure?
It is to see my dividends coming in."
— John D. Rockefeller

A Rich Man's Pearl of Wisdom #3
"I make money while I sleep."

A group of visitors came to see a famous wealthy man, anxious to learn how he had become financially independent. The group was ushered into the great hall to meet this well-to-do figure, who was dressed in a colorful bedroom robe.

One of the visitors stepped forward and asked, "Sir, tell us how you became so wealthy, while the rest of us remain so poor?"

The rich man smiled, and then said, "I'll tell you my little secret to success on one condition — you must promise never to tell a soul." They all agreed.

He walked over to a couch and sat down, making himself comfortable. He poured a drink and then, in a solemn whisper, he said, "Here's the secret: *I make money while I sleep!*"

The crowd of listeners looked perplexed, so the millionaire explained.

"All of you work hard for a living and make money while you are awake, do you not?" he asked. They all nodded. "But the secret to financial success," said the man, "is to make money while you are asleep."

"But how can we make money while we're asleep — that's impossible," one curious visitor responded.

"It's very simple," said the rich man. "You must search and find someone who will pay you while you sleep, when you are not working! All of you are used to paying others for the things you want in life. All you have to do now is find someone willing to pay something in return."

"But we don't know anyone like that," said another visitor. "Who in their right mind would do such a foolish thing?"

"You are right," continued the wealthy man, sipping his drink. "Most people won't do it. The grocer won't pay you for sleeping. Neither will your landlord. Nor will your boss at work. But, fortunately, there are a few persons who will pay you while you sleep."

"Who? Who?" the audience demanded impatiently.

"Well," the millionaire responded, leaning back in his recliner. "There's the banker downtown. He pays me interest while I sleep. There's the president of the local utility company, he pays me a dividend check every quarter. There's the legal offices that lease my building on Second Avenue, they pay me rent every month. There's the CEO of a gold mining company I own shares in, he pays me capital gains while I sleep. Why, just today, I received a considerable sum of money from these sources, all sent through the mail last night, while I slept."

"And you did nothing in return?" asked someone.

"That's right," declared the independent man. "I didn't work one minute for any of them.

All I did was lend them some of my surplus wealth, or I invested in one of their companies, or I leased them one of my buildings, and in return they pay me for the privilege of using my money or my building. I am therefore making money all the time, not just during the day."

"Tell us," a visitor asked inquisitively. "How can we be like you?"

"It's very simple," answered the man. "All you need to do is lend these institutions some of your hard-earned income and savings, or invest your money in a building or rental property, and it won't be long before you too will be making money while you sleep."

Then, he rose from his chair. The interview was over. He gave one word of warning. "But, remember, if you spend all your income, or go into debt, you won't have any money to lend and invest, and you'll never make money while you sleep. Consequently, you will never be financially independent."

Inside Information

"To speculate without being an insider
is like buying cows in the moonlight."
— Daniel Drew

"You can't pick cherries
with your back to the tree."
— J. P. Morgan

"Out of the room, out of the deal."
— Peter Brown
Vancouver promoter

"The dealers on Wall Street
could make huge fortunes
if only they had no inside information."
— John Maynard Keynes

"Good companies buy their own stock."
— Michael Sheimo

"There are many reasons to sell a stock,
but only one reason to buy."
— Anonymous

Hot Tips

"Hot tips usually result in cold feet."
— BERT DOHMEN

"There's only one sure tip from a broker:
the margin call."
— JESSE LIVERMORE

"Acting on an 'inside' tip will break a man
more quickly than famine, pestilence,
crop failures, or accidents."
— EDWIN LEFEVRE

"Assume you're always the last to know."
— CHARLES KIRK

Beating the Market

"You can win a horse race,
but you can't beat the races."
— EDWIN LEFEVRE

"A swallow a summer doesn't make."

"One Robin doesn't make a spring."
— ANONYMOUS

(one winning stock doesn't mean you will
beat the market over the long term)

"In the world of investing,
being average means you are
one of the best students in the class."
— ROBERT R. JULIAN

"Investment managers are not beating the
market. The market is beating them."
— CHARLES ELLIS

"Neat systems for beating the market
and formulas for getting rich
are almost always fraudulent."
— GERALD LOEB

"The efficient market theory means
that short-run changes in stock prices
cannot be predicted.
Investment advisory services, earnings
predictions, and complicated chart patterns,
are useless . . .
Taken to its logical extreme,
it means that a blindfolded monkey
throwing darts at a newspaper's
financial pages could select a portfolio
that would do just as well
as one carefully selected by the experts."
— BURTON G. MALKIEL
A Random Walk Down Wall Street

"Most people are beaten up by the market
instead of beating the market."
— MARK T. HEBNER

"When it's in the papers, it's in the price."
— BILL MILLER (Legg Mason)

Making it Big in the Stock Market

"Winners win big."
— Jesse Livermore

"Go big or go home."
— Robert Bishop
(surfing phrase)

"The way to make big money is to be right at exactly the right time."
— Edwin Lefevre

"To make big money,
you have to bet on the unexpected."
— George Soros

"When we see something that makes sense,
we act very fast and very big."
— Warren Buffett

"The big money is not in the buying
and the selling, but in the sitting."
— Jesse Livermore

"Don't look for small gains.
With the right issue, you should
be able to double your money."
— GERALD LOEB

"To double your money in a year, you have to
bet on what people don't know that's true."
— MARK SKOUSEN

"It takes courage to be a pig. When you're
right on something, you can't own enough."
— GEORGE SOROS

"May your investments be like
the capital of Ireland, always Dublin!"
— ANONYMOUS

Story of a Big-Time Operator

Trader to broker:
"Buy XYZ stock."

Broker to trader:
"How many shares?"

Trader to broker:
"Buy 'til you move the market."

Investing in Real Estate

"Want to make a million dollars?
Borrow a million dollars and pay it off."
— JACK MILLER
as told to John Schaub

"Invest in land.
They aren't making any more of it."
— WILL ROGERS

"Never invest in anything that
eats or needs repainting."
— BILLY ROSE
(1899-1966)
composer and entrepreneur

Successful Investing

"Good investing is simple:
buy a good asset at a good price
and hold it for a good long time."
— ADRIAN DAY

"I don't want a lot of good investments;
I want a few outstanding ones."
— PHILIP A. FISHER

"The great majority are not going to be able
to successfully invest or speculate."
— GERALD LOEB

"The typical investor has usually gathered a
good deal of half-truths, misconceptions, and
just plain bunk about successful investing."
— PHILIP A. FISHER

"Successful investing is anticipating
the anticipations of others."
— JOHN MAYNARD KEYNES

"Few [traders] gain sufficient experience in
Wall Street to command success until they
reach that period in life in which they have
one foot in the grave."
— HENRY CLEWS
Fifty Years on Wall Street

It's easy to grin
when your ships come in
and you've got the stock market beat,
but the man worth while
is the man who can smile
when his pants are too tight in the seat.
— ANONYMOUS

"You can have the top 20%
and the bottom 20%.
I'll take the middle."
— BARON ROTHSCHILD

"I will tell you my secret: I never buy at the
bottom and I always sell too soon."
— BARON NATHAN ROTHSCHILD
(quoted in *Reminiscences of a Stock Operator*)

"It's not whether you are right or wrong,
but how much money you make
when you're right,
and how much you lose when you're wrong."
— GEORGE SOROS

"All sunshine makes a desert."
— OLD ARAB SAYING

"Making it and keeping it
are two different things."
— ANONYMOUS

"It requires a great deal of boldness and a great
deal of caution to make a large fortune,
and when you have it, you require ten times
as much wit to keep it."
— NATHAN ROTHSCHILD

"Everyone has the brainpower to follow the
stock market. If you made it through
fifth-grade math, you can do it."
— PETER LYNCH

"Successful investing requires humility."
— JOHN TEMPLETON

"The art of investing is being able
to adjust to change."
— GERALD LOEB

"If you have the cool nerves of a great
gambler, the sixth sense of a clairvoyant,
and the courage of a lion,
you have a ghost of a chance
of making money in the stock market."
— BERNARD BARUCH

"Successful investing requires a Spartan
attitude, a warrior attitude in which feelings
are kept on hold. As William Blake wrote in
The Marriage of Heaven and Hell,
'Joy laughs not! Sorrows weep not!'"
— LOWELL MILLER

"We should treat market truisms
with respect but not as gospel."
— DICK DAVIS

"Believe half of what you see, none of what you hear, and everything that you feel."
— KAREN GIBBS

"The single most important lesson that I've learned is that thinking is just rehearsing. You must learn to act."
— DICK RUSSELL

"I am wrong nine out of ten times but it is what I do in consequence of being right that has made my fortune."
— GEORGE SOROS

"Investment success accrues not so much to the brilliant as to the disciplined."
— WILLIAM J. BERNSTEIN

"The best investor is a social scientist."
— MICHAEL MILKEN

"Success has ruined many a man."
— BEN FRANKLIN

On Being Rich

"The years roll round and the last will comes;
when I would rather have it said,
He lived usefully, than, *he died rich.*"
— BENJAMIN FRANKLIN

"Those who have earned the greatest wealth
have not always earned
the greatest happiness."
— B. C. FORBES

F. Scott Fitzgerald: *The rich are different* than
you and me.
Ernest Hemingway: *Yes, they have more money.*

Money may be the husk of things,
but not the kernel.
It gives you food, but not appetite.
Medicine, but not health.
Acquaintances, but not friends.
Servants, but not faithfulness.
Days of joy, but not peace or happiness.
— HENRIK IBSEN

A Rich Man's Pearl of Wisdom #4:
A Young Man Take a Journey

A young man was planning a long journey across the desert. Before he left, a wise old man came to him and said, "Half way through your trip, you will come to an oasis where you'll find some pebbles on the ground. When you are ready to leave, pick up some of these pebbles and put them in your saddle. When you finish your journey, you will be both happy and sad."

The young man smiled in disbelief.

"Promise me you will do this!" the old man insisted.

The young man didn't quite understand, but he took the old man's advice and went his way. The trip was long and hard. Finally he arrived at the oasis. He was tired, and so was his camel, who headed straight for the water hole. After a day of relaxation, eating and drinking, it was time to move on. As he approached his camel, he remembered the strange request by his mentor, and dutifully reached down to pick up a handful of pebbles, put them in his bag and continued his journey.

When he arrives at his destination, he unloaded his saddle bags, and suddenly remembered the little bag of pebbles. He reached into his pocket, and was much surprised to find that his pebbles had turned into valuable rubies.

As he reflected on the wise man's promise, he realized that he truly was both happy and sad. Happy because the pebbles were now rubies, but sad that he didn't pick up more of them!

My wife Jo Ann says that the parable is about having children. Growing up, they often act like rough pebbles, but when they are fully grown, they are often like jewels. When you come to the end of life's journey, you are grateful for those you have, but sorry you didn't have more.

But I think the parable also has merit in the

world of investing. If you make money, you are both happy and sad. Happy that you made money, but sad because you didn't invest more.

You can never be completely happy as an investor. If you lose money, you wish you hadn't invested. If you make money, you wish you had invested more.

As the old poem goes:

> Sell them and you'll be sorry,
> Buy them and you'll regret,
> Hold them and you'll worry,
> Do nothing and you'll fret.

———

"Money doesn't buy you happiness.
I now have $50 million, but I was just as happy when I had $48 million."
— ARNOLD SCHWARZENEGGER

Bernard Baruch's
10 Rules of Investing

In his memoirs, Baruch listed his 10 rules of investing in a chapter entitled "My Investment Philosophy." The rules are worth applying today.

1. Don't speculate unless you can make it a full-time job.

2. Beware of barbers, beauticians, and waiters bringing gifts of "inside" information or "tips."

3. Before you buy a security, find out everything you can about the company, its management and competitors, its earnings and possibilities for growth.

4. Don't try to buy at the bottom and sell at the top. This can't be done--except by liars.

5. Learn how to take your losses quickly and cleanly. Don't expect to be right all the time. If you have made a mistake, cut your losses as quickly as possible.

6. Don't buy too many different securities. Better have only a few investments which can be watched.

7. Make a periodic reappraisal of all your investments to see whether changing developments have altered their prospects.

8. Study your tax position to know when you can sell to greatest advantage.

9. Always keep a good part of your capital in a cash reserve. Never invest all your funds.

10. Don't try to be a jack of all investments. Stick to the field you know best.

Ten Ways to Lose Money on Wall Street

By Humphrey Neill
"The Market Cynic"

1. Put your trust in boardroom gossip.
2. Believe everything you hear, especially tips.
3. If you don't know — guess.
4. Follow the public.
5. Be impatient.
6. Greedily hang on for the top eighth.
7. Trade on thin margins.
8. Hold to your opinion, right or wrong.
9. Never stay out of the market.
10. Accept small profits and large losses.

From *Tape Reading and Market Tactics*, by Humphrey B. Neill (Trader's Library, 1931), p. 102.

14 Simple Truths

By Larry Swedroe

Truth 1: Active Investing Is a Loser's Game:
It Must Be So

Truth 2: The Past Performance of an Actively
Managed Fund Is a Very Poor
Predictor of Its Future Performance

Truth 3: If Skilled Professionals Don't
Succeed, It Is Unlikely That
Individual Investors Will

Truth 4: The Interests of Wall Street and the
Financial Media Are Not Aligned
with Those of Investors

Truth 5: Risk and Reward Are Related:
Great Companies Provide Low
Expected Returns

Truth 6: The Price You Pay Matters

Truth 7: The Most Likely Way to Achieve
Above Average Returns Is to Stop
Trying to Beat the Market

Truth 8: Buying Individual Stocks and Sector
Funds Is Speculating, Not Investing

Truth 9: Reversion to the Mean of Earnings
Growth Rates Is One of the Most
Powerful Forces in the Universe

Truth 10: The Forecasts of Market Strategists
and Analysts Have No Value,
Except as Entertainment

Truth 11: Taxes Are Often the Largest Expense
Investors Incur

Truth 12: Knowledge of Financial History Is
Critical to Successful Investing

Truth 13: Adding International Assets to a
Portfolio Reduces Risk

Truth 14: There Is No One Right Portfolio,
but There Is One That Is Right for
You

From *The Successful Investor Today*, by Larry Swedroe
(2003)

"Succeeding as an investor takes a strong mind
– and a strong heart."

— JASON ZWEIG

Dennis Gartman's
20 Rules of Trading

To trade successfully, think like a fundamentalist, trade like a technician – It is imperative that we understand the fundamentals driving the trade, but that we understand the market's technicals also. Then, and only then, can we, or should we, trade.

Trade like a mercenary guerrilla – Our duty is to fight on the winning side, to be willing to change sides immediately upon detecting that the other has gained the upper hand, and to deploy our capital (both mental and monetary) on that side. Of the two types of capital, the mental is the more important and expensive of the two.

The objective is not to buy low and sell high, but to buy high and to sell higher – We cannot know what price is low. Nor can we know what price is high. We can, however,

have a modest, reasonable chance at knowing what the trend is and acting upon that
trend.

In bull markets we can only be long or neutral
– And in bear markets we can only be short
or neutral. That may seem self-evident, it is
not, however.

**Markets can remain illogical far longer than
we can remain solvent** – According to our
good friend, Dr. A. Gary Shilling. There is
wisdom in knowing that illogic often reigns.
Markets are often enormously inefficient
despite what the academics have believed,
and return to rationality immediately upon
forcing us to exit a position.

**Sell markets that show the greatest signs of
weakness, and buy those markets that
show the greatest strength** – Metaphori-
cally, when bearish we need to throw our
rocks into the wettest paper sacks, for they
break most readily. In bull markets, we need

to ride upon the strongest winds . . . they
shall carry us higher than lesser ones.

**Resist the urge to trade against the consensus
too early** – The consensus may be wrong at
major turning points, but it is right and can
remain right for long periods of time in the
midst of a great move. Patience, rather than
impatience, is far better when considering
any trade.

Try to trade the first day of a gap (either higher or lower) for gaps usually indicate violent new action – We have come to respect
"gaps" in our twenty-five years of watching
markets; however in the world of twenty-
four hour trading, they are becoming less
and less important, especially in forex dealing. Nonetheless, when they happen (especially in stocks) they are usually very important.

Trading runs in cycles, some good, most bad
– Trade large and aggressively when trading

well, trade small and modestly when trading poorly. In *good times*, even errors are profitable, in *bad times*, even the most well researched trades go awry. This is the nature of trading, accept it.

Margin calls are the market's way of telling you that your analysis and position taking are wrong – Never meet a margin call… liquidate.

Never, ever under any circumstance add to a losing position – Not ever, not ever! No more need be said; to do otherwise is illogical.

Respect outside reversals after bull or bear runs – Reversal days on the charts signal the final exhaustion of the bullish or bearish forces that drove the market previously. Respect them. We may not wish to reverse our position, but we must at minimum learn to avoid trading in the old trend's direction. And even more important shal be the respect paid to weekly and the even more rare, montlhy, reversals. Pay heed!

Keep your technical systems simple – Complicated systems breed confusion, simplicity breeds elegance.

Respect and embrace the very normal 50% to 62% retracements that take prices back to major trends – If a trend is missed, wait patiently for the retracement. Draw a box on the chart, between those levels and watch how often prices retrace to that box, then act.

Know that in trading/investing an understanding of mass psychology is often more important than an understanding of economics – Most, or at least much of the time.

Establish initial positions on strength in bull markets and on weakness in bear markets – The first addition should also be added on strength as the market shows the trend to be working. Henceforth, subsequent additions are to be added on retracements.

Bear markets are more violent than bull markets – And so also their retracements.

Be patient with winning trades, be enormously impatient with losing trades.

Understand that the market is the sum total of the knowledge and wisdom of all – If we learn nothing more than that, we have learned very much indeed.

Finally, all rules are meant to be broken – The trick is knowing when... and how infrequently this rule may be invoked!

List of 15 Nevers

"Never answer a margin call."
— HUMPHREY NEILL

"Never convert a convertible."

"Never ask a barber if you need a haircut."

"Never panic."
— J. PAUL GETTY

"Never let a profit turn into a loss."
— Mark Skousen

"Never short a dull market."
— OLD TRADER'S ADAGE

"Never day trade — ever."
— CHARLES ELLIS

"Never let taxes get in the way of profits."

"Never invest in anything
you don't understand."
— PETER LYNCH

"Never short the trend."

"Never fight the Fed."
— LARRY KUDLOW

"Never make the big mistake."
— WARREN BUFFETT

"Never leave to chance what you can
achieve through calculation."
— CARDINAL RICHELIEU

"Never forget — things change."
— LOWELL MILLER

"Never invest in any idea
you can't illustrate with a crayon."
— PETER LYNCH

My Favorite J. P. Morgan Story

"The man who is a bear on the future of the
United States will always go broke."
— J. P. MORGAN
(1895)

One final story: In the early years of the
Twentieth Century, when J. P. Morgan ruled
Wall Street, a visitor came to the City. He was
a long-time friend of Morgan, a commodity
trader from Chicago. He was what might be
called a "perma bear" following the Panic of
1907. No matter how high or low the stock
market went, his outlook was pessimistic.
Another crash, panic, and depression were just
around the corner.

This was his first visit to the world's
greatest city. He arrived at 23 Wall Street, and
was ushered into J. P.'s spacious office over
looking the Exchange on one side and George
Washington's statue on the other.

They immediately began talking about the markets, Morgan being bullish as ever, and his commodity friend being bearish as ever. "J. P.," he said, "the news oversees doesn't look too good."

"A buying opportunity!" responded Morgan.

After an hour of friendly disputing about the markets, Morgan invited his guest to join him for lunch. They walked outside and started moving up toward Broadway. As they did so, his friend couldn't help but admire the skyscrapers the dotted that Manhattan horizon. Morgan gave him a tour of the giant buildings, pointing out the Singer Building, the Woolworth Building across from City Hall, the famous three-sided Flatiron Building, and the recently completed Met Life Tower, rising 50 stories high, the tallest skyscraper in the world at the time.

His friend was duly impressed. He said he had never seen anything like it, not even in Chicago.

Finally, J. P. Morgan stopped his friend, and said, "Funny thing about these skyscrapers. Not a single one was built by a bear!"

THE EXTRA - ORDINARY LIFE OF WARREN G. HARDAWAY

A Short Story by Mark Skousen

Warren G. Hardaway was an ordinary stockbroker in every way. He worked at 23 Wall Street, across the street from the New York Stock Exchange, in the old J. P. Morgan offices. The year was '09.

Hardaway was a midwesterner, in his late-twenties, a business graduate from Harding College in Arkansas (not to be confused with Harvard College in Massachusetts), and had begun working a few years back for J. P. Morgan. He got the job almost by luck. On a job search in New York, taking a train down into the City, he met a Morgan stockbroker who was impressed with Hardaway's style and helped him land a job at the prestigious firm. "You look like a Morgan man," he said.

For the next two years, Hardaway's performance was run-of-the-mill. Like most brokers, he underperformed the market averages. He started out knowing almost nothing about finding winning stocks. Following the advice of the most senior of the stockbrokers, Irving Tuttle, who told him "the best way to learn how to invest is to invest," he bought stocks for clients almost randomly. His superiors complained that his sales were doing poorly, and cautioned him that he needed to get better results, or he might be let go. Still he was friendly, and other brokers liked him. They would spend time at a bar on Wall Street after the markets closed, go to baseball games, and hang out together. He dated occasionally, but being the quiet, modest kind, living alone in a small apartment off Union Square, he often went weeks without a date.

But Hardaway harbored a secret side to his life that gave him some excitement. He subscribed to a few offbeat magazines like Hot Rod, Rifleman, Popular Mechanics, and

National Inquirer. He often responded to bizarre ads in the magazines. One ad promised 1,000% a year profits by identifying the exact top and bottom of every market using Japanese Candlesticks and bar charts. Being a novice and not knowing how to pick winning stocks consistently, he could use that. He sent in his $99, but the reports proved entirely unsuccessful. Veteran Irv told him, "only failure teaches success." Hardaway's stock picks for clients still underperformed the market indexes.

Another ad promised a simple 200-day moving average. "Forget fundamentals — earnings, cash flow, and book value," warned the ad. "Main Street doesn't work on Wall Street." The solution? "Just look! Follow the line on the 200-day moving average chart," the report advised. So Hardaway did, and it worked for a while. Then without warning the market blew up, his system stopped working, and he kept getting whipsawed. Irv explained, "No system works forever."

Finally, Warren asked Irv, "What's your formula for success?"

"Simple," he replied. "Invest based on value, not popularity."

"What's value?"

"Ah, only experience can teach you that." And Irving walked away.

Still, Hardaway was hooked on the ads. Another time he saw a full-page advertisement from an astrologer: "Send me your birthdate and I'll predict your death date! Absolutely guaranteed, or your money back!" The ad included several testimonials of the relatives of the deceased who confirmed the soothsayer's ability to predict when individuals would breathe their last. Hardaway was skeptical, but curiosity got the best of him again — he had often wondered if he would live a long life, or die early — and he finally sent in his $25. The check cleared, but after waiting a few months, he gave up on getting a response. He wrote a letter of complaint to the post office, but that was the end of it.

Another time he bought a booklet, "How to Pick Up Girls," based on an ad that promised effective pick-ups lines and a men's cologne that women couldn't resist. He sent in $49, but neither the pick-up lines nor the perfume worked at a local bar.

"That's the last time I'll be fooled," he thought.

In the ensuing weeks, the market turned ugly, and the dollar fell sharply overseas, igniting a big sell off in the Dow, and by late September, Wall Street was teetering toward a full-scale crash. Everyone expected it in October, but it came early. "Expect the unexpected," Irv commented. Hardaway was caught completely by surprise, and his clients were fully invested in high tech stocks and other "go go" speculations when the market started falling. He received numerous complaints from his clients, who threatened to close their accounts. Some did. His superiors expressed displeasure with the closing of these accounts, and again warned him that if he didn't keep his clients happy, he would be let go.

He sought advice, but all Irv said was, "Troubled waters make for good fishing."

The Federal Reserve intervened, injecting more money into the banking system and cutting interest rates, and finally the market turned around in October. Hardaway and his clients were relieved when their accounts rebounded.

He now had something to look forward to as his 30th birthday approached on October 23.

On that Wednesday, as lunchtime approached, suddenly a dozen brokers surrounded his desk, and gave him a birthday party. He was indeed surprised. He didn't think any of them knew his birthday, but Alex Bakerfield, his colleague to his right, had told them and they all took him out to lunch. He had a great time, and felt for the first time that he was fitting in, at least socially. Yet he still wondered if his job was in jeopardy given his poor performance at Morgan.

When he returned to his desk, he had another birthday surprise. One of the brokers had placed on his desk one of those gag newspapers — it was a Wall Street Journal with the headline, WARREN FUND HITS ALL TIME HIGH FOR BILLIONAIRE HARDAWAY. The issue was dated Wednesday, October 23, in the year '29. Warren Hardaway smiled broadly as he read the cover story:

New York, New York: On his 50th birthday, Warren G. Hardaway, the world's weathiest man and founder of the Warren Fund, had much to celebrate. He enjoyed his best year since the famous closed-end fund was created eighteen years ago. The Warren Fund more than tripled in value, while the Dow Jones Industrial Average rose tepidly by eight percent.

"We are pleased with our performance," Mr. Hardaway said modestly in an interview yesterday at his Hampton estate, where he was preparing to entertain some friends and family celebrating his half-century mark. "But I'm concerned that investors will think this trend will continue — I doubt if we can maintain this kind of above average returns."

In fact, the Warren Fund has been so popular that the premium on the investment fund has risen to 67% above the estimated book value this year, the highest of any fund on Wall Street. Stocks and private investments currently listed in his fund have been a carefully guarded secret, though he has failed to keep imitators from creating clones that duplicate his winning portfolio.

The Journal continued to report that Mr. Hardaway had planned a special announcement on his birthday, but the article didn't say what it was. The story continued on to another page inside the Journal, but he had read enough to have a good laugh. He turned to his colleague Alex, and asked, "Hey, which one of you guys came up with this fake newspaper?" Alex looked at the newspaper, laughed, and then shook his head. "Beats me, but I love the headline."

Warren took back the paper, laid it on his desk, and got back to work checking his messages and watching the stock market screen. The market was up again. A telephone call came in from one of his clients. While he was talking, he again picked up the fake newspaper. A headline at the bottom of the front page caught his eye, and he mumbled to himself, "Boy, we'd be in real trouble if that happened!" The headline read, "20th Anniversary Memorial Service Planned for London Nuclear Explosion." The story described a nuclear attack in London, the action of a Indonesian terrorist group, twenty years earlier.

"Not funny," Warren thought, "even for a gag paper. This newspaper is full of crazy fantasies," Warren thought as he tossed the newspaper into the wastepaper basket, cleaned off his desk and headed out the door.

That evening he called his parents and went out to dinner with a couple of friends at a local restaurant in Greenwich Village. He didn't get home until midnight.

The next morning he awoke at his normal 7 am, and turned on the TV, his head swimming from a long night out. Was he hearing the right words? He sat in utter shock as the TV reporter announced that a rogue terrorist group had exploded a nuclear device in London, killing over a million inhabitants. It was the worst terrorist attack in history. He couldn't believe it. His thoughts raced along, wondering "Who will be hit next? New York? Washington? Shanghai? What will this mean to the stock market, my job, my clients?" A crash is inevitable, he thought. The market will be closed for weeks. This may mean his career will be wiped out. He thought, if only I had invested in some gold to protect my clients….and me! He quickly got dressed and ran out the door.

On the subway on his way to downtown Wall Street, it hit him. The fake newspaper! It couldn't be, but somehow, someway, it had predicted the nuclear attack in London. Hey, maybe that special issue of the Wall Street Journal wasn't a gag after all. It might be some mysterious augur of the future — 20 years from now. It might be worth something. It might reveal a lot more about events over the next 20 years. "I must go back and retrieve that paper," he thought.

Then it hit him again. Where was that newspaper? Oh, no, it's gone! I threw it away!

But, he thought again, maybe it's still there. Maybe the cleaning lady didn't empty the wastepaper basket yet.

He jumped off the subway, ran up to his office at 23 Wall Street, leaped up the stairs, and pushed his way through a crowd of rowdy brokers to his desk, out of breath. He stared.

Damn! The basket was empty. He sank into

his chair in despair, not recognizing the chaotic voices of other brokers around him. Will Wall Street be shut down? The brokers waited for a call from their boss...and the President of the United States.

But wait, his mind raced. Maybe he could retrieve the paper from the central garbage unit of the building. The garbage trucks may not have come by yet. Maybe, just maybe, the newspaper was still here in the building and hadn't been picked up by the garbage truck. It's worth a try. He ran down to the basement and demanded, "Where are the garbage bags from last night?" He looked around, and somebody said, "They've gone outside. The garbage truck comes this morning to pick them up."

Warren ran outside.....and saw the garbage truck leaving. He shouted, "Wait! Wait!" But it was too late. The truck pulled away. He mentally noted the number of the truck, jumped into a cab and said, "Follow that truck!" Finally, after chasing it down for several miles, he got the truck driver to pull over. "This is an emergency," Hardaway explained with great emotion. "I need to go through the garbage and search for a missing paper — it's a matter of life or death."

The driver refused. "No way," he said.

"But it has to do with the London nuclear attack! You've got to let me find that paper, or I'll call the police!"

The driver ignored him, and kept driving to the city garbage dump. Hardaway followed him, jumped out of the taxi, and started rummaging through the trash as the truck emptied the garbage. He went through bag after bag. Finally, after several hours of searching, and just as he was about to give up in despair, Hardaway suddenly spied the special edition of the newspaper halfway outside an open black bag. He pulled it out safely and stared at it.

"Hallelujah!" he exclaimed as he clutched the paper.

He took the newspaper back to his apartment — no way was he going to take it to JP Morgan offices — and started looking it over more carefully. He first read the story on the 20th anniversary of the nuclear explosion, and compared the report closely to what he was hearing on the television. Everything matched perfectly except for the alleged perpetrators. Today's reports from London said it was Middle East terrorists. He didn't know what to think about the gag newsletter — was it real?

A few days later, he found out. It came out that the terrorists were Indonesian radicals, just as his futuristic newspaper had reported.

That gave him more confidence that the newspaper was somehow real, an actual edition of the Wall Street Journal dated October 23 of '29. Over the next few days, he examined the Journal paper carefully, all 90 pages.

He still had doubts. Was it real, or just a fluke?

Fortunately, the paper on page 48 mentioned another event that was to occur in a few months, on December 21 in '09 —

the bankruptcy of world's biggest bank, whose headquarters were in London, precipitated by the nuclear attack. He waited patiently. Sure enough, on December 21, the newspapers around the world reported the bankruptcy as front page news.

Once again the newspaper was vindicated.

At this point Warren Hardaway began to think how he might profit from this futurist newspaper. After all, this was a Wall Street Journal that contained the closing prices of thousands of stocks, both here and abroad, as well as the price of bonds, commodities, and mutual funds, near the end of the year '29.

How could he, an ordinary stockbroker who had underperformed year after year, take advantage of this data?

Could 20 years into the future help him make investment decisions *now*?

Maybe it could, but it didn't seem possible. Perhaps the paper would help him 20 years from now, but today? A lot of crazy things —

bull markets, bear markets, panics and crashes, another nuclear attack — could happen between now and then.

Then it dawned on him. He could start by looking through the stock listings and see the names of new companies, companies whose names didn't exist in today's listings. Maybe he could patiently wait for when these new companies appeared as IPOs, and based on their future price in '29, he could judge whether they were the next IBM or next Microsoft. It might work.

He started with the 30 Dow Industrials, which the Journal always listed daily in a separate table, to see if any new companies had been added to the list in 20 years. He figured that new companies that made the Dow 30 must have been incredibly successful to make the list of the top 30 richest companies in America.

There were quite a few changes, but one company stood out, called Jackson

Technologies. It must have invented some incredible new technology to make the Dow 30, he thought to himself, but he would have to wait to find out what it was.

He didn't have to wait long. The market finally started recovering from the London nuclear attack, although the turnaround was slow for fear there might be another explosion in a major city around the world. Fortunately, nothing happened, and the global markets gradually returned to normalcy.

A year later he read in the papers about a new IPO called Jackson Resources. Was this the same company as the new Dow addition, Jackson Technologies? Maybe. Jackson was a mining company. He took his chances and recommended it to his clients. It fizzled. Its primary mine in Mexico turned out to be a dud, and the stock price fell by 50% even though commodities were rising in price. Irv said, "You can't make big money without taking big risks." But more clients left and J. P. Morgan executives were losing their patience with stockbroker Warren G. Hardaway.

But within a year things changed at Jackson Resources. A scientist at Jackson discovered a breakthrough in nanotechnology, the micro-processing of commodities that would allow Jackson Resources to expand manufacturing into a whole new retail market — cosmetics, fuel cells, semi-conductors, and other productive uses. The scientist had made a major breakthrough, discovering an advanced fuel cell that had multiple uses in transportation, including cars that could now run on batteries. As revenues started coming in, the company decided to change its name to Jackson Technologies. The stock took off, rising 1000% in two years.

Fortunately, many of Hardaway's clients still held Jackson Resources, now Jackson Technologies, in their portfolios, and Hardaway had even bought a thousand shares himself. He and his clients were suddenly rich.

The '29 Journal looked like a goldmine. He

kept a photocopy at home, safely hidden away, while he kept the original in a safe deposit box, and kept its existence a secret. He never told anyone – not his boss, not his colleagues, not his parents, not his girl friends.

According to the price of Jackson Technologies in the '29 newspaper, it was clear that the stock had a bright future even after rising 1000%. After all, it still had a long ways to go before it would be listed in the Dow Jones Industrial Average. He refused to take profits, and encouraged his clients to add to their accounts. The stock fell sharply at times, but he held on, reminding his clients that stocks never move in a straight line, and the stock price continued to hit new highs. Warren Hardaway was finally getting some recognition in the firm, and most importantly, new clients were coming on board. But most of his colleagues and superiors at Morgan thought the Jackson pick was a fluke. As one broker opined, "Even a blind squirrel finds a nut sometimes."

Hardaway decided it was time to see if

there were other chestnuts in this special issue. He went through the entire list of stocks and underlined every company that wasn't listed in the '29 Journal. When they went public, he would check the price, compare the price in '29, and decide whether to add it to his recommended list.

Of course, he wasn't sure how significant the '29 prices were in real terms, after twenty years of inflation. But it was better than nothing.

With his success in Jackson Technologies, Hardaway decided to focus exclusively on new issues. Of the hundreds of IPOs coming out each year, how would he choose? He decided to limit himself to those that came public that year and were still listed in the '29 Journal at substantially higher prices. By the year '10, he had identified a dozen such companies, and recommended them to his clients. Not all of them worked out immediately. Some fell in price, but the majority skyrocketed by several hundred percentage points, and kept moving higher. He also missed out on some big winners, new issues that were eventually acquired by larger companies, and therefore not listed separately on the exchange in '29. As Irv said, "You can't kiss all the pretty girls." But overall his success rate was extremely high in an area that is often associated with high risk; most IPOs sell for less than their original price after two years.

It wasn't long before Warren G. Hardaway was relatively famous as the IPO guru, and market analysts and the financial media started paying attention to his stock picks. His client list began growing rapidly, and he found himself being interviewed on more and more financial networks. He started writing a high-priced newsletter, "The Warren Report," containing his latest recommendations and comments on the markets.

In the year '11, he decided it was time to start his own investment company, and make it closed-end, issuing a limited number of shares that he could control. In an open-end mutual funds, new investors could overwhelm him and force him to buy his favorite stocks at prices far beyond their real value. By creating a closed-end fund, he could have complete control of the fund, what he would buy, and when, without being unduly pressured by speculators.

Choosing the name of the fund was easy. The '29 Wall Street Journal had chosen it for him: The Warren Fund. J. P. Morgan was the primary investment banker, and the fund began with a sizeable investment of $100 million. Hardaway himself owned 20% of the company, worth $20 million.

The IPO was a huge success, sold out immediately, and went to a premium on the first day.

As the years went by, Warren Hardaway felt he could be more aggressive. He knew where stock prices were now, and what they would be in '29, but what about in between? It was still an educated guess that would become more educated with time.

His approach in the Warren Fund was to

stick to IPOs which appeared to be blockbuster performers, based on their prices in '29. Often his choices appeared at first to be a big mistake, but they always made huge come backs. He took comfort in one of Irving's sayings, "The best investments are often those that look dead wrong when they are made." He often leveraged his position. The Warren Fund was volatile, but the long run trend was clearly above the averages, with annual returns of 20%, 30%, and sometimes 90%. He had a few losing years, but the total return was spectacular.

After the fund reached $1 billion in value by the year '19, and his net worth exceeded $200 million, he decided to go independent. He quit his job at J. P. Morgan and, despite every effort to keep him, he set up his own offices on Long Island, where he ran the Warren Fund.

Being a multi-millionaire also solved his dating problem. He was surrounded by women who suddenly found him attractive. But he chose wisely, a pretty brunette in her twenties who was also from the Midwest named Debra

Brooks. They met at Brown University, where he was delivering a lecture, and they married in '19. Over the next ten years, she gave birth to two boys and a girl, and they raised their family in the Hamptons.

During this time, Hardaway diversified his portfolio to include stocks that did well, according to his reading of his singular source, and occasionally to short stocks that he thought might fall sharply in price between then and '29. Commodities like oil and gold, corporate and government bonds, and foreign stocks were all added to his buy list.

Again, he was often proved wrong in the short term, and suffered a down year occasionally. Stocks that he shorted sometimes went up, and stocks he bought went down. But he stuck with his choices and was eventually vindicated. He quoted from an old book on Wall Street borrowed from Irving, "Remember, the big money is not in the buying and selling, but in the waiting."

One particularly egregious mistake involved an IPO that he thought should be a ten-bagger, but it never went anywhere. It opened at $5 a share, then collapsed to $1 a share. How did it reach $10 a share, as the '29 Journal quoted? Was it was all a deception? A few years later the company did a 10-to-1 reverse stock split to attract institutional investors. Institutions are prohibited from buying stock under $5, so what to do? Do a reverse stock split. As a result, the stock went instantly from $1 to $10 a share, but the fundamentals of the company didn't change. He was misled by the $10 price in the '29 Journal. Fortunately, it was only one of over 250 stocks in his fund, so it didn't hurt its performance much. Hardaway wasn't fooled too often by such Wall Street shenanigans, and the fund's value continued to rise every year, far more than the funds of any other money manager or mutual fund.

Hardaway also decided to start investing personally in some of the companies before they went public, if he could discover their company names in the '29 Journal. By investing early, he received insider stock, and sometimes warrants and options that paid off handsomely. But he was smart enough to realize he didn't have any particular skill in running those new businesses. He left that up to the company officers and founders.

Nothing *exceeds* like success on Wall Street, as Irv said, and by time the year '25 came, the Warren Fund had broken all records as the top mutual fund in the country. *Money* magazine said that $10,000 invested in the Warren Fund was worth over $1 million in ten years. The public clamored to buy his company on the stock exchange, and the premium above the estimated value exceeded 100% at times (no one knew for sure what the book value was, since the Warren Fund included private companies). Hardaway was constantly inundated with requests for interviews, speeches, and honorary degrees. The president of the New York Stock Exchange urged him to relieve the pressure by issuing more shares. He resisted, but as an act of good will, he created a second, albeit lower priced, closed-end fund, The Warren Fund II, with an initial investment of $50 billion. By '25, the two Warren Funds were worth over $100 billion, and due to his own stake in the two funds, plus the managing of his own personal accounts and business interests, Warren G. Hardaway was now on the Forbes list of the 400 Richest People in America. His children now required a chauffeur and body guard to and from grade school.

As the 29th year approached, Hardaway began thinking more and more of what his next strategy would be. The day of reckoning would soon be upon him and his much touted Warren Funds. What to do after October 23 of '29? He walked along the beach in front of his Hampton estate, pondering his next move. He felt a little bit like Superman, who in one episode suddenly lost all his magical powers. After '29, he would no longer be Superman. Not knowing the events and prices after the year '29, would he return to his ordinary performance as a stockbroker, which meant *under*performing the market? Sure, he had learned a lot about investing over the past 21 years, but did he have the guts and sheer skill to really beat the market? He has his doubts. What if he had a couple of down years? What would people think? He could switch to a variety of stock index funds, but even that would tarnish the image he had developed so carefully as a man who could consistently beat the markets, at least in the past decade.

No, there was only one thing to do: Announce his retirement on his 50th birthday, October 23 in the year '29. He would choose a successor and retire forever from Wall Street and keep intact his reputation as the world's greatest investor, never to return. He would devote the rest of his life to philanthropy, gardening, art collecting, travel, and being an ambassador of peace and good will. Maybe he would establish a foundation to fight the spread of nuclear weapons. (Luckily, he thought, no nuclear explosions had occurred since the London bombing in '09.) He read the autobiographies of Andrew Carnegie, J. Paul Getty, Bill Gates, and other giants of industry. They all diversified into other activities and causes. He would do likewise. He told his wife and she approved. "Now that's a great way to celebrate your 50th birthday, Warren," she exclaimed. It was time for Warren Hardaway to spend more time with his family, she said, and to take a break for his 14-hour work days.

He spent the next few months quietly and carefully selecting his successor among a half dozen trusted group managers in the Warren Funds, without informing any of them when and who would be the lucky choice. Hardaway was still young enough that rumors about a successor never developed.

Warren Hardaway had his PR office send out a press release announcing a special event on his 50th birthday. Everyone, including his staff and managers, was invited. The night before, he selected his successor, his long-time colleague, Alex Bakerfield — after the market had closed.

The fateful day came and he was especially excited to see the Wall Street Journal that day. Sure enough, when he picked up the newspaper at home early Wednesday morning, he smiled as he looked at the exact same headline: WARREN FUND HITS ALL TIME HIGH FOR BILLIONAIRE HARDAWAY.

The newspaper was exactly the same as the one he had in his safe deposit box. He could destroy it now and no one would be the wiser.

The press conference was held at the New York Stock Exchange at 10 o'clock. The room was packed with reporters and television cameras. As he read his shareholder letter of resignation as founder and CEO of the Warren Funds, and introduced Alex Bakerfield as the successor, a gasp went through the crowd. They were all instantly dialing their cell phones spreading the bad news.

The reverberations were felt immediately on Wall Street and all the global markets.

Stocks fell sharply all day long, but the pressure on the Warren Funds was the most dramatic. With the premiums on the fund at over 67%, the funds sold off dramatically, and by the end of the day, the fund had lost more than 70% of its value. The premium had been completely wiped out, and for the first time ever, the two Warren Funds sold at a discount — all in one day.

Hardaway expected some kind of sell off, but a crash? This was too much. He had become a prisoner of his own success. His retirement plans were threatening his own reputation. He sought comfort with his wife and family, but he grew more nervous during the day as the markets continue to swing madly. What to do?

That afternoon, Warren Hardaway was besieged at his offices in Long Island by reporters and angry shareholders, demanding that he appear and issue some kind of a statement to reassure investors that all would be well with the Warren Funds under new management.

Finally, after the market closed, he appeared before a large group of animated reporters and furious investors. They shouted questions and obscenities, and he tried to calm the crowd. A man dressed in an old suit stepped forward, his eyes intense, his hand shaking, and moved quickly toward Hardaway. Suddenly he reached into his jacket and pulled out a revolver....

The next day — dated October 24 of '29 — the front page of the Wall Street Journal ran an even most shocking headline:

WORLD'S RICHEST MAN SHOT TO DEATH

FOLLOWING RESIGNATION AND STOCK MARKET CRASH

New York, New York: A lone gunman, identified by police as Pitman Fitzgerald, shot and killed Warren G. Hardaway, the world's richest man, at an afternoon news conference following his announcement of his resignation as manager of the Warren Fund. The announcement set off a stock market crash around the world, and the Warren Fund fell 70% in value yesterday. Mr. Fitzgerald was believed to be a major shareholder in Mr. Hardaway's fund. He is being held by New York police on a charge of first-degree murder. No bail has been set.

One of the bystanders at the Hardaway press conference was an older gentleman who stood clutching a magazine ad. He seemed intensely interested in the proceedings and Hardaway's surprise announcement. The ad was old and crinkled. The headline read, "Send me your birth date and I'll predict your death date! Absolutely guaranteed, or your money back!"

MY FAVORITE BOOKS ON WALL STREET

Mystery Men of Wall Street, by Earl Sparling (New York: Greenberg Publisher, 1930)

100 Minds That Made the Market, by Ken Fisher (Business Classics, 1995)

Reminiscences of a Stock Operator, by Edwin Lefevre (Wiley & Sons, 1994, 1923)

How to Be Rich, by J. Paul Getty (Playboy Press, 1965) — as contrasted with "How to Get Rich" by Donald Trump.

Richest Man in Babylon, by George S. Clason (1926)

The Battle for Investment Survival, by Gerald M. Loeb (Simon & Schuster, 1965)

Where are the Customers' Yachts?, or a Good Hard Look at Wall Street, by Fred Schwed Jr. (Wiley, 1995, 1955)

The Plungers and the Peacocks, by Dana L. Thomas (New York: G. P. Putnam's Sons, 1967)

Fifty Years in Wall Street, by Henry Clews (New York: Irving Publishing Co. 1908) — Be sure to read the notorious chapter, "Women on speculation"

Extraordinary Popular Delusions and the Madness of Crowds, by Charles McKay (1841)

Conservative Investors Sleep Well, by Philip A. Fisher (Harper & Row, 1975)

Dividends Don't Lie, by Geraldine Weiss (Longman, 1990)

Why Most Investors Are Wrong Most of the Time, William X. Scheinman (Fraser Publishing, 1991)

The Art of Contrary Thinking, by Humphrey B. Neill (Caxton Press, 1963)

The Lore and Legends of Wall Street, by Robert M. Sharpe (Dow Jones Irwin, 1989)

Good Source for Quotes and Insights

Stock Traders Almanac (Wiley & Sons): Updated annually by Jeffrey and Yale Hirsch, with daily quotes and financial information: www. stocktradersalmanac.com.

About Mark Skousen

Mark Skousen, Ph. D., is a professional economist, investment expert, university professor, and author of over 25 books. He was recently ranked by SuperScholar.org as one of the top 20 most influential economists today. He earned his Ph. D. in monetary economics at George Washington University in 1977. Currently he is a Presidential Fellow at Chapman University in California. He has taught economics and finance at Columbia Business School, Columbia University, Barnard College, Mercy College, and Rollins College. Over the years, he has been a consultant to

IBM, Hutchinson Technology, and other Fortune 500 companies.

Since 1980, Skousen has been editor in chief of *Forecasts & Strategies*, a popular award-winning investment newsletter. He is also editor of three trading services, Skousen Private Equity Trader; High Income Alert; and Fast Money Alert. In 1995, he served as editor of the investment series, "Secrets of the Great Investors," with Louis Rukeyser as narrator.

He is a former analyst for the Central Intelligence Agency, a columnist to *Forbes* magazine, and past president of the Foundation for Economic Education (FEE) in New York. He has been a columnist for *Forbes* magazine (1997-2001), and has written articles for *The Wall Street Journal, Liberty, Reason, Human Events, the Daily Caller, Christian Science Monitor,* and *The Journal of Economic Perspectives.* He has appeared on ABC News, CNBC Power Lunch, CNN, Fox News, and C-SPAN Book TV. In 2008-09, he appeared as a regular weekly guest on Kudlow & Co. on CNBC.

His economic bestsellers include *Economics*

on Trial (Irwin, 1991), *Puzzles and Paradoxes on Economics* (Edward Elgar, 1997), *The Making of Modern Economics* (M. E. Sharpe, 2001), *The Big Three in Economics* (M. E. Sharpe, 2007), *EconoPower* (Wiley, 2008), and *Economic Logic* (Capital Press, 2000, 2013). In 2009, *The Making of Modern Economics* won the Choice Book Award for Outstanding Academic Title.

Based on his work *The Structure of Production* (NYU Press, 1990, 2015), the federal government began publishing in Spring 2014 a broader, more accurate measure of the economy, Gross Ouput (GO), every quarter along with GDP.

His financial bestsellers include *The Complete Guide to Financial Privacy* (Simon & Schuster, 1983), *High Finance on a Low Budget* (Bantam, 1981), co-authored with his wife Jo Ann, *Scrooge Investing* (Little Brown, 1995; McGraw Hill, 1999), and *Investing in One Lesson* (Regnery, 2007). His latest book is *A Viennese Waltz Down Wall Street: Austrian Economics for Investors* (Laissez Faire Books, 2013).

In 2006, he compiled and edited *The Compleated Autobiography, by Benjamin Franklin* (Regnery).

He is the producer of *FreedomFest*, "the world's largest gathering in free minds," every July in Las Vegas.

In honor of his work in economics, finance and management, Grantham University renamed its business school, "Mark Skousen School of Business."

Dr. Skousen has lived in eight nations, and traveled and lectured throughout the United States and in 77 countries. He grew up in Portland, Oregon. He and his wife, Jo Ann, and five children have lived in Washington, DC; Nassau, the Bahamas; London, England; Orlando, Florida; New York; and California.

Websites:
www.mskousen.com
www.markskousen.com
www.freedomfest.com

Email:
markskousen@skousenpub.com

INDEX

Index